Praise for
REAL COLL

"If you read and use this book, your college journey will be much happier and more productive. Every student affairs office should recommend it."
>—Loren Pope, author of *Colleges That Change Lives* and *Looking Beyond the Ivy League*

"Stone and Tippett address serious, substantive, and challenging issues with deep psychological wisdom. This book is superb "must" reading for any student on the brink of college life and any parent seeking an understanding of what college holds in store for their maturing daughters and sons."
>—Charles Ducey, Ph.D., Director, Bureau of Study Counsel, Harvard's Center for Psychological and Learning Services

ABOUT THE AUTHORS

DOUGLAS STONE worked for many years as a residential and academic advisor at Harvard College, and with students and administrators at The Citadel in South Carolina, on issues of communication, gender, and culture. A Lecturer on Law at Harvard Law School, he is coauthor of the best-selling *Difficult Conversations: How to Discuss What Matters Most*, which has been translated into eighteen languages. Doug has taught and mediated in South Africa, Colombia, and Cyprus, and at the World Health Organization, and his articles have appeared in *The New York Times, Parents, Glamour,* and *Real Simple.* He has also consulted to groups working on race relations, organ donation, gun control, and crisis counseling for survivors of rape and sexual assault. A partner at the corporate education firm Triad Consulting, Doug is a graduate of Brown University and Harvard Law School. In his spare time, he plays basketball and writes supposedly funny screenplays. Doug can be reached at dstone@post.harvard.edu.

As a Harvard College student, **ELIZABETH TIPPETT** was the founding director of a mediation program designed to help students resolve roommate and other conflicts. For her senior thesis, she surveyed hundreds of college students in an effort to understand why and when they decide whether to seek help for mental health concerns. Through her work with the Harvard Negotiation Project, Liz served as a teaching assistant for Harvard Law School's negotiation course, and developed the Project's forthcoming Web site, which documents its international peace-building activities over the last two decades. Liz is currently a Harvard Law School student. She spent last summer working for International Bridges to Justice, a human rights organization dedicated to improving legal services in China. She grew up in Beaumont, Alberta, Canada. Liz can be reached at tippett@post.harvard.edu.

Real
College

The Essential Guide
to Student Life

DOUGLAS STONE and
ELIZABETH TIPPETT

PENGUIN BOOKS

PENGUIN BOOKS
Published by the Penguin Group
Penguin Group (USA) Inc., 375 Hudson Street,
New York, New York 10014, U.S.A.
Penguin Group (Canada), 10 Alcorn Avenue, Toronto, Ontario,
Canada M4V 3B2 (a division of Pearson Penguin Canada Inc.)
Penguin Books Ltd, 80 Strand, London WC2R 0RL, England
Penguin Ireland, 25 St. Stephen's Green, Dublin 2, Ireland
(a division of Penguin Books Ltd)
Penguin Group (Australia), 250 Camberwell Road, Camberwell,
Victoria 3124, Australia (a division of Pearson Australia Group Pty Ltd)
Penguin Books India Pvt Ltd, 11 Community Centre, Panchsheel Park,
New Delhi — 110 017, India
Penguin Group (NZ), cnr Airborne and Rosedale Roads, Albany,
Auckland 1310, New Zealand (a division of Pearson New Zealand Ltd)
Penguin Books (South Africa) (Pty) Ltd, 24 Sturdee Avenue, Rosebank,
Johannesburg 2196, South Africa

Penguin Books Ltd, Registered Offices:
80 Strand, London WC2R 0RL, England

First published in Penguin Books 2004

10 9 8 7 6 5 4 3 2

LIBRARY OF CONGRESS CATALOGING-IN-PUBLICATION DATA

Stone, Douglas, 1958–
Real college : the uncensored guide to student life /
Douglas Stone and Elizabeth Tippett.
p. cm.

ISBN 0-14-303425-1

1. College students—United States—Conduct of life.   2. College environment—
United States.   I. Tippett, Elizabeth, 1980–   II. Title.

LA229.S645 2004   378.1'98'0973—dc22   2004044636

Printed in the United States of America
Set in New Caledonia
Designed by BTDNYC

TO OUR PARENTS,

Anne and Don Stone and Mitsu Oishi and Clay Tippett,

who taught us everything

To Ete Anderson,
Good luck with
the class of 2010!
Best wishes,
E Tippett

Acknowledgments

F irst, a huge thanks to all the college students we've worked with over the years—for all the challenges we've faced and victories we've shared, and all that we learned together. This book comes mostly from our experiences with you.

It was while working with our friend Elizabeth Kopelman Borgwart on a project to help college roommates manage their differences that many of the ideas in this book first began to take shape. Now a professor of history, Liz is the very model of what it means to truly care about your students. She inspires us all.

Our colleagues at the Harvard Negotiation Project— Roger Fisher, Linda Kluz, and Daniel Shapiro—were an endless source of ideas and feedback, cheerfully absorbing our whining and complaints while offering only encouragement and optimism in return.

We owe a great debt to Charlie Ducey, Director of Harvard's Bureau of Study Counsel for his wise guidance, and to his colleagues. Over the years, the Bureau has advised and assisted thousands of students with their most difficult challenges, and has taken the lead in figuring out what really helps. A special thanks to Ariel Phillips, also of the Bureau, who taught us the importance of "listening first" when someone is in trouble; and to Michael Hoyt, Richard Kadison, and their extraordinary colleagues at the University Health Services.

During Doug's seven years as an academic and residential advisor, the Freshman Dean's Office at Harvard College was like a second home. Doug fondly recalls many formative conversations with his mentor Hank Moses (former Dean of Freshman and currently Headmaster at the Trinity School in New York), Dean Ibby Studley Nathans, Karen Heath, Ginger MacKay-Smith, Lisa Harris, and the late Burris Young. Hank's outstanding book *Inside College: New Freedom, New Responsibility* is elegantly written, packed with helpful advice, and well worth tracking down.

We also wish to acknowledge our dear friend and colleague, the late Archie Epps, former Dean of Students at Harvard College. Archie, your spirit enlivens this book, and you are deeply missed.

Thanks to cofounders of the Harvard Conflict Resource Center, Naomi Coquillon and Travis Batty, as well as the many other diligent friends, colleagues, and administrators who got the program off the ground.

With deep gratitude for your time, energy, and wisdom, we acknowledge those friends and colleagues who read draft chapters and offered feedback. We were going to write a page about each of you, but one of you advised that names were enough: Christina Araiza, Ashley Bauman, Wynn Calder, Sylvie Carr, Tracy Anne Chung, Naomi Coquillon, Ben Edelman, Chris Edmonds-Waters, Robin Ely, Travis Good, Elizabeth Greene, Alpana Gupta, Louisa Hackett, Joyce Heen, Holly Holloway, Sarah Hurwitz, Onyi Iweala, Jeffrey Kerr, Jessie Kerr, Agnes Li, Mike Melcer, Erica Michelstein, Jackie Parker, Alan Price, Michael Riera, Don Rubenstein, Katelyn Rubenstein, Gabriella Salvatore, Jody Scheier, Roman Sokolowski, Karen

Tenenbaum, Jen Thompson, Nancy Tran, Graeme Truelove, Erin Wallace, Joe Wolfe, Marie Wolfe, and Jim Young. Maybe one day we'll have a party so you can all meet each other.

A special shout-out to our friends who came to Matt and Luanne's cookout last August—yes, Bloss and Faulks, you too—and for the book titles that were generated there, including obvious winners like *And Now We Are Freshmen* and *I Miss My Mommy and My Roommate Smells Like Ass*.

Our pal Michael Mah deserves credit for introducing us to the concept of the "dreaded J Curve" cited in the Studying chapter; props to Debbie Goldstein, whiz-bang writer and all-around puncher upper, for adding needed spice to the chapter on Relationships; and thanks to Gina Scaramella, Executive Director of the Boston Area Rape Crisis Center, for her expert advice on the material on rape and sexual assault.

Uber-agent and friend Esther Newberg, along with her colleagues at ICM, did a great job in helping to nurture this book along, and for that we say, "Go Huskies!" Our editors at Penguin, Jane von Mehren and Jennifer Ehmann, did more work on this book than we or they had any reason to anticipate. But the book is a thousand times better for it, even if we still chose on occasion to start a sentence with "but," and use the third person "they" and "them," etc., to refer to indefinite singular antecedents as a way to maintain gender neutrality. Thank you for your sure-handed editing and patient guidance, and most of all, thank you for challenging us. Please, no more push-ups.

Thanks to our siblings: Liz's twin brother and best bud, Ben Tippett, whose finest contributions to the book were felled by the ax of good taste; and Doug's siblings, Randy Stone, Robbie Blackett, and Julie Doherty—a funnier, more loving trio no brother has ever had.

Finally, thank you to Sheila Heen and John Richardson, who not only fed and entertained us pretty much every night while this book was being written, but provided key feedback and support in the clutch. Sheila, who is also Doug's business partner, took on many of Doug's other work obligations when the book overwhelmed. Sheila, you are simply the best.

DOUG AND LIZ
Cambridge, Massachusetts, 2004

Contents

Introduction

Now that you've skipped ahead and read the chapter on Sex, you probably have a pretty good sense for how this book works. We follow four fictional students during their freshman year of college, and offer advice on how they can deal with the challenges they face. These students seem to have more problems than most, and their instincts for dealing with them aren't always stellar. But that's the point. This book isn't for the perfect, blemish-free students you see on TV or find sitting under trees in admissions brochures. It's for real students. As exhilarating and fulfilling as college can be, real students face real challenges.

Real students have conflicts with their roommates, parents, and friends. They enjoy some classes and not others, procrastinate, and get addicted to video games. Real students get bored and depressed, and don't always have exciting plans for Saturday night. They feel insecure about relationships and sex, face hard choices about drinking and drugs, and struggle with eating issues and body image—or have friends who do. Real students aren't always sure who they are, where they fit in, or what they want to do with the four years ahead of them, let alone the rest of their lives.

Despite it all, or perhaps because of it, real students wouldn't trade their college experiences for anything.

The advice, tools, and ideas we offer come from our work over the years with countless college students—and from our own experiences as students. Our goal throughout is to help you understand the binds, tensions, and thoughts that get in the way of doing what makes sense in the first place, and to offer practical, easy-to-follow advice. Whether you're caught in the panic of trying to find someone—anyone—you know in the dining hall, the disappointment of a bad grade, or the hopeful confusion of an ambiguously flirtatious e-mail, we will help you through.

HERE'S SOME BACKGROUND on the characters we will visit in the book. There's Macani, a freshman from Ohio who put on an all-dog version of the play *Cats* during senior week and is working hard to maintain a long-distance relationship with her high-school boyfriend, Craig. She shares a room with PJ, a recruited rower who grew up with her sister and divorced mother in New York.

Across the hall is Rollo, from California. He has a passion for physics and chess, although his love of writing complaint letters to strangers is still a mystery to his parents. His roommate, Sweeney, served two terms as student council president of his Tennessee high school and proved remarkably effective given his perfect record of never attending a meeting. He often e-mails his trusted vice president and best pal, Duncan, who was one of only seven black students at this school. Duncan goes to college back in Tennessee. You'll get to know these students, along with some of their friends, as their year proceeds.

Welcome to college. Enjoy the ride.

Real

College

Roommates

From: Rollo
To: Mega Posters Online
Sent: Wednesday, September 8, 5:09 PM
Subject: in stock?

To whom it may concern:

I recently purchased a poster of Dr. Richard Feynman, who just
took over the number three spot on my all-time favorite
physicists list. I think many of his equations are super-good.
At any rate, my roommate took down my Feynman poster, and
instead insists on a poster of someone named Oktoberfest
Girl. In the spirit of compromise, I wonder whether you have a
poster of Dr. Feynman posing with Ms. Girl? If not, might you
have pictures of Ms. Girl near a particle accelerator?

Best, Rollo

YOUR VERY OWN ROOMMATE

When you get to college, there are constant reminders that you're in a different world. Foremost among them is your roommate. Having a roommate doesn't seem like a foreign concept until the day you move in. Then it becomes clear that the person you'll be living with isn't so much your "mate" as a "complete stranger," and the space you are sharing isn't so much a "room" as a "walk-in closet."

Your roommate won't be a stranger for long, of course, and could turn out to be incredibly cool. They might be just like you, or totally different in all the best ways.

But what if your roommate isn't so cool? What if they turn out to be really loud or kind of stinky? What if they hate you for no reason, or worse, hate you for a good reason?

Living with a roommate can be tough. In this chapter, we'll help you get things started off right and give you tools for getting your roommate situation back on track when things go wrong.

Be Wary of First Impressions

It's normal to make snap judgments when you first meet someone. Here's what Macani wrote to Craig, her boyfriend from home, after meeting her roommate.

From: Macani
To: Craig
Sent: Thursday, September 2, 5:09 PM
Subject: roomies

Hey Craig,
I met the roomie this morning! Her name is PJ. She's just like she was on the phone, except that when we talked this summer she failed to alert me to the fact that she's insanely attractive, athletic, confident, and wealthy. And, who knows, probably some sort of math genius. We're like two peas in a pod. Jealous? Moi?

But I'm not sure she has an actual personality. She told me she "does crew," and then she asked what I "do." For some reason not even known to me, I said, "beauty pageants." I was like "ha, ha," but she didn't laugh.

I don't know, Craig, it's not looking good. I'm afraid to unpack my SpongeBob beanbag chair. What if she doesn't "get" that either?

Macani

Go ahead and have your first impressions. But remember, people don't always act like themselves when they're nervous or in a new environment. Your first impressions, as Macani demonstrates, can be as much about your own worries and insecurities as about what the other person is like. If you put too much stock in those initial judgments, it will be harder to see your roommates for who they really are, once things settle down.

Your Roommate Is Not a Message from the College

Here's PJ's e-mail to her mom after meeting Macani.

From: PJ
To: Mom
Sent: Thursday, September 2, 9:55 PM
Subject: rooming conspiracy?

Hi Mom,
Just met my roommate. She seems pretty nice. She's really smart. I think she might have graduated first in her class or something. She's sort of small, and said she's half Italian and half Japanese. Oh, and this is sort of interesting—she does beauty pageants.

But I'm a little worried that they didn't put me with any other athletes. A lot of the other girls in crew said they were either rooming with another athlete or there were a bunch in their dorms. But I'm sort of off by myself. Maybe they don't think I'm going to last?

Love,
PJ

Students often wonder what their roommate pairing "means." Why didn't the college put me with another athlete? Does the fact that my roommate is gay (or straight) mean they assumed I was gay (or straight)? Shouldn't I be with other pre-meds? What were they trying to tell me by putting me with a girl who, like me, is overweight? What, in short, does my roommate say about me?

Nothing.

Some colleges put roommates together almost randomly, looking only at practical factors like whether you smoke and when you go to bed. Other schools match people with great care, but it's mostly a matter of intuition, and there's a ton of randomness at play. Sexual orientation, economic background, social style, politics, religion, and practically anything else about who you are and how you see yourself are rarely considered.

Remember, everyone has to live somewhere, and the puzzle of who lives with whom can be solved by a billion possible combinations. Your roommate is not a message from anyone.

Good Roommates Don't Have to Be Good Friends

You can be great roommates with someone you don't particularly like, and you can be miserable roommates with someone you do.

It's nice if you and your roommate become friends, but it's icing on the cake. Your first priority is to live well together, which means sharing a small space without getting in each other's way. Even if your roommate is Dr. Evil, you could still have a perfectly pleasant living situation, so long as his evil ways don't interfere with your life, and your life doesn't interfere with his evil ways.

As we'll see, Macani and PJ turn out to be good friends, but more important, they are good roommates.

YOUR VERY OWN ROOMMATE CONFLICT

All roommates, even those who get along great, are going to have their differences. Having a good rooming situation doesn't mean there are no conflicts. It means you're doing your best to deal with those conflicts before they get out of hand.

What causes conflict? Here are some common factors.

The "You're Annoying Me *on Purpose*" Fallacy

Nothing escalates conflict faster than the assumption that your roommate is not just annoying you, but annoying you *on purpose*. If you lived near a rumbling subway, it might bother you initially, but after a few weeks you'd find that the noise virtually disappears.

Noise from a roommate is different, because *you* respond differently. Instead of thinking, "That's a loud noise," you think, "That's a loud noise *coming from my roommate*. I've asked her to be quiet, but she doesn't care. She's selfish and thoughtless, and does this on purpose to annoy me!" Because it's coming from your roommate, the noise seems ten times louder.

But is your roommate actually being annoying on purpose? It's an easy assumption to make, especially if you're anxious or tired. And, of course, jerks happen, and sometimes they happen to be your roommate.

But you can also imagine other explanations for what's going on. Maybe your roommate isn't as sensitive to noise as you are and doesn't realize how much it's affecting you. Maybe she's trying to be quieter but forgets on occasion. Maybe when *she's* under stress, she gets "social" and loud.

Even if one of these explanations is true, your roommate is still responsible for her behavior. But the more you think your roommate is annoying you on purpose rather than unintentionally, the more aggravating the noise becomes. And the more aggravated you are, the less likely you are to handle the problem well.

Of course, your roommate might also be grappling with the "on purpose" fallacy—about you.

From: Sweeney
To: Duncan
Sent: Monday, September 6, 2:00 AM
Subject: Seizure robot roommate

Dunk,

Top Four Ways My Roommate Is Trying to Mess with Me
1. Turned our room into *Star Trek* meets *Lord of the Rings* meets *No Sex Ever*.
2. When I asked him if he wanted to go out on Friday he said his "copy of *Nerd & Driver* magazine just arrived." How about later? "No, I better stay here in case next week's issue gets delivered early."
3. He won't tell me how to pronounce his name. Every time I call him Roh-lo, he says it's supposed to be Rahhh-lo. And later he says it's the other way around.
4. Made me turn down my earphones. EARphones.

Does he actually come up with this stuff himself, or is he following some manual?

Sweeney

As you can see, it's complicated. Next time you find yourself seething over an annoying roommate, stop to consider what else might be going on for them. Before you talk to them, force yourself to think of at least two reasons other than "just to annoy me" for why they're doing what they're doing.

The "My Way Is Normal, Your Way Is Weird" Fallacy

You and your roommate each have certain habits in life, certain ways you like to operate. They relate to everything—when to go to sleep, how long to spend in the shower, how loud to play music. You may not even be aware of all your preferences, until your roommate shows up and does things differently.

It could be that your roommate is actually odd, but most differences aren't due to that. Some things are just a matter of personal taste. Sweeney likes posters of scantily clad women. Rollo likes inspirational physicists. Other preferences come from the way things were done when you were growing up. If you shared a room with your sister, you might be used to sharing all your stuff with her. If your roommate is an only child, she might be shocked to find her CDs out of order and some of her shampoo missing. In her family, her stuff was *her* stuff.

Or maybe you had visitors to your house all the time. It was a meeting place for anyone who wanted to stop by. Your roommate's house wasn't and so it bugs him that your friends are always coming over unannounced.

Some differences go beyond mere preference and are partly physiological. You can sleep through anything; your roommate wakes up at the slightest sound. You need fresh air;

your roommate gets cold easily. You like the smell of perfume; your roommate is allergic.

Similarly, different things trigger anxiety in different people. You can't sleep if you think the door is unlocked; your roommate could care less. You can't study if the room isn't neat; your roommate doesn't even notice. People also have different routines to unwind. Sweeney decompresses by getting out and socializing; Rollo relaxes by playing computer games.

Whatever your differences, the better you understand where they come from, the less likely you are to jump to the conclusion that your roommate is just weird, selfish, or difficult.

We All React to Conflict Differently

You and your roommate might have totally different ways of handling conflict, and that in itself can cause conflict. Your own tendency might be to try to avoid confrontation. When something bothers you, you try either to ignore the problem or send an indirect message. You might be thinking, "When is my roommate going to realize that I'm unhappy with her? Hasn't she noticed that I haven't asked her to go to dinner with me in three weeks? Why does she continue to be so inconsiderate?"

The answer might be that your roommate hasn't noticed. Her conflict style is different. When she's unhappy, she's direct. And she's been assuming you're the same way. She's thinking that since you haven't said anything, everything must be great between you.

People also differ on what conflict means. In some families, loud arguments are common and can be a way of showing affection: "I wouldn't fight with you if I didn't care." In other families, such arguments are rarer, and when they happen, it can feel extremely threatening.

This is why one roommate can report that things are great while the other reports that there's constant tension. It may be that they're both right—from their own points of view.

THE DO-IT-YOURSELF GUIDE TO FIXING ROOMMATE CONFLICT

The tension in Sweeney and Rollo's room came to a head in early October, and in a moment of less than stellar behavior, Rollo ripped up two of Sweeney's posters. Later that evening, Sweeney confronted him.

Sweeney: Dude, what shit is this!? Why did you rip up Oktoberfest Girl and Nurse Twins? What is the problem with you? That was a fucked thing to do.

Rollo: No, it wasn't.

Sweeney: No, it wasn't?! How can you honestly say that wasn't a fucked thing to do?

Rollo: You deserve it.

Sweeney: Dude, this is so wrong. Living with you is like living in some convent with Trekkie nuns. You're in here studying all the time and I can never have any friends over. I have to listen to music in the corner at volume minus seven. I should get an award for putting up with this.

Rollo: You're right, you're the perfect roommate.

Sweeney: Can you seriously say that I ever impose on you *at all*?

Rollo: Would you like my response as a haiku, or as an
   alphabetical list?

Sweeney: How about as money for my posters?

Rollo: You've had it in for me since the moment I got here. You
   don't respect me or my things. You ripped down my one
   poster—

Sweeney: —that was my friend Cube—

Rollo: —you spill beer on my problem sets, you show up drunk
   at two in the morning—

Sweeney: —we're in college—

Rollo: —You probably don't even remember stepping on my
   Atari last night. Here's the haiku: You are such an ass. Cube
   is such an ass as well. So leave me alone.

Was this fight inevitable? Despite all the ways that Rollo
and Sweeney are different, the answer is no. If they had followed the five guidelines below, this confrontation could have
been avoided. Though it won't be easy, if they start now,
there's still plenty of time for them to work things out.

1. Clarify the Rules of the Room

Setting up some explicit guidelines to live by at the beginning
of the year is crucial. That advice might seem strange. You
might figure that good roommates don't need to talk about
that stuff, but the opposite is true. Good roommates are good
roommates because they *do* talk. In fact, the conversation itself can be as important as whatever rules you come up with.
It gets you talking about how you're going to live together, and
makes it clear what you each care about.

Guidelines can relate to anything that involves sharing
the same space and living together. Here are some simple ex-

amples: "Snacks on the top shelf of the mini-fridge are for whoever buys them. Snacks on the other shelf are for whoever's hungry." "It's okay to use my shampoo, but don't use my towel." "We each agree to raise problems as they come up, before they turn into big issues."

Of course, most dorms also have guidelines for how to live together in a community, and you and your roommate should live within these. Appealing to community guidelines is actually a good way to raise a difficult issue, because it makes the problem less personal: "It's not me, it's the rule."

2. Look for Easy Compromises

Often small compromises allow each of you to get most of what you want. If loud music bothers you, identify blocks of time when it's okay to turn up the volume, and blocks of "quiet time" when the volume should be low or the music turned off altogether. High-volume blocks might be Fridays and Saturdays, or any day up until 9:00 p.m., or anytime your roommate wants to have friends over if he asks first. Instead of having an all-or-nothing rule, the goal is to divide things up so that each of you gets some of what you care about most.

Sometimes bundling together different interests can help you find compromises. If you're in a suite of rooms, for example, whoever gets to keep the single room an extra month might have additional cleaning duties, or the other roommates might be allowed shower priority. The more things you put on the table, the more ideas you can come up with.

If you're not sure how a particular rule is going to work out, have a trial period. In fact, it's a good idea to check in periodically on how everything in the room is going; stick with what works and change what doesn't.

3. Be a Good Roommate Yourself

"What kind of advice is that!? My *roommate* is the problem, not me!" Well, even if you're right, showing a little respect for your roommate is as good for you as it is for your roommate. But what does "respect" mean, beyond some vague generalization? Here are three concrete actions that make a huge difference.

Consult first. This one guideline can change your whole year: before you decide anything that impacts the room or your roommate, talk to them. Don't grab the best bed before your roommate shows up. Don't change the furniture without discussing your plan. Don't have friends over late at night without first getting your roommate's permission or, at a minimum, letting them know about it in advance. In short, remember that you have a roommate. If you want to do something that might affect them, talk to them first.

Don't issue commands. If you want to listen to music and your roommate is studying, don't order your roommate to "put up with the music or leave." Make it open for discussion: "Hey, can you study with music on? If not, let's figure out what makes sense." The same thing applies when the tables are turned. If you want to study when your roommate is listening to music, don't order them to turn it off. Instead, say, "Hey, I'm having trouble concentrating with the music. Let's figure it out."

Be generous. Like you, your roommate will endure periods of more than normal stress. Midterms, big games, romantic problems, loneliness. When big stressors hit, be generous.

From: Sweeney
To: Duncan
Sent: Friday, October 29, 8:34 PM
Subject: my ankle, my roommate

Hey Dunk,

So, I'm playing some pickup at the gym last night and I twist my ankle. I limp home in excruciating pain, and Rollo tells me I have to get ice on it. We don't have ice, so he goes to the 24-hour store and gets like seven bags. And he also gets me the new issue of *Football Times,* two packs of Hostess cupcakes, and a bag of shrimp-flavored crackers. They actually tasted good. You should try them.
  I'm starting to think he's a good guy, in his own weird way.

Sweeney

Forget the rules. Let your roommate have the room to study or to stay up late talking with a friend. You may not know just what they're going through, but there's never a downside to generosity. And one day, you may need the favor returned.

4. Stick Up for Yourself

You might be doing everything right. You've talked with your roommate about how you want to live together and have set out some rules for the room. You've bent over backward to treat your roommate with respect. But you aren't getting the respect you deserve in return. If that's the case, it's time to stick up for yourself.

Remember, it's your room too. Sticking up for yourself is first and foremost about attitude. You have to know in your heart and mind that you deserve to be at this school and in this room as much as anyone else, including your roommate.

It doesn't matter who's bigger or stronger, who's wealthier or more popular. It doesn't matter where you're from or what activities you do. It doesn't matter whether you got in off the waiting list or were an early admit. You have the right to feel comfortable in your own room, and to raise any concerns you have that cause you to feel otherwise. The room belongs to *both* of you.

Bring it up. Sticking up for yourself isn't *only* about attitude. You also have to raise what's on your mind. And that's not easy.

If you wanted to start a fight with your roommate, what would you do? You'd toss out an accusation or two, maybe attack their character. They'll get all defensive, and before you know it, you're in a useless argument.

But what if you *don't* want to start a fight? Are there ways to get started that "cause" good conversations? Nothing is surefire, but here are a few examples of what to try and what to avoid:

MORE HELPFUL	LESS HELPFUL
POINTING OUT DIFFERENCES "Since we have such different lifestyles, maybe we can work something out so we're less in each other's way."	**ACCUSATIONS** "Just because you don't care about flunking out doesn't mean I don't care about flunking out!"
HOW IT'S AFFECTING YOU "You probably don't know this, but a bunch of times I've had to dry the floor off after you get out of the shower."	**RHETORICAL QUESTIONS** "Why do you have to be such a slob? Would it kill you to wipe off the floor after you take a shower?"
A BETTER SYSTEM "We should probably figure out a better system for dealing with garbage. Our 'he who tops it off, drops it off' policy isn't working out so well."	**BRING IT ON** "You're just waiting to see how long I can go without taking out the trash, aren't you? Well, you don't know how much trash I can take!"

The basic idea is to raise your concerns honestly, but in a way that doesn't automatically put the blame on your roommate. The key move is this. Instead of saying, *"You're wrong. What are you going to do about it?"* you're saying, *"We're different. What can we do about it?"*

As you notice from the examples, lightness and humor can help. But don't be afraid to let your roommate know when something really matters to you. You can do this just by putting it out there: "Hey, I don't want you not to be able to have your boyfriend visit. But it's important to me to talk about it in advance. It really matters to me. The room belongs to both of us, so I need to have some say."

From: Macani
To: PJ
Sent: Wednesday, November 3, 4:35 PM
Subject: stuff

Hey PJ,

I know this is a really lame thing to put in an e-mail, because you're the "put everything out in the open" roommate, and I'm the pathetic passive-aggressive roommate. Anyway, uh, it's your turn to vacuum. I did it last week because you were off at a regatta, but I can't do it this week because I have two papers due. Maybe this sounds all petty and stuff, but I just wanted to bring this up before I got all whacked about it.

Or, I don't know, maybe that's not it at all. Maybe I'm just trying to find a way to say I miss you since you're away so much. No, actually, I guess it's also the vacuuming.

I don't know. Anyway, I do miss you. And our room is a mess.

Macani

Hear them out. It may be that when you raise a concern your roommate immediately says, "You're right, I'll change." More likely they'll defend themselves or point out why you're wrong. Either way, try to hear them out.

That's probably annoying advice, especially if you're the "good one" in the dispute. But the truth is that if you listen to your roommate's concerns, they're more likely to listen to yours. If they're upset or frustrated, they won't be able to pay much attention to what you want. If they feel like you've heard their concern and care about it, they'll have some space in their head to listen to what's going on with you.

One tip on listening: translate your roommate's accusations or attacks into legitimate concerns. If they call you an asshole, you don't need to debate the point. You know you're not technically an asshole, and they know you're not technically an asshole. Instead, assume they're upset, and ask about it: "Hey, sounds like you're pissed at me. What's the matter?" And then, actually listen.

5. If It's Really Bad, Get Help

You might be thinking, "So, it's all good advice. But none of it will work for me because my roommate isn't just a little bit from Hell, my roommate is the Lord of the Underworld."

A couple thoughts here. First, don't be that kind of roommate yourself. Don't threaten your roommate or get violent. Ever. That's not only a roommate problem, that's a life problem.

Even if your roommate is totally out of line, don't respond in kind. Don't say, "Oh yeah, you think you can kick my ass?! Let's see you try!" It's just not worth getting thrown out of school because of your roommate's anger problems.

Instead, disengage. If you have to, get out of your room and go somewhere else—to a friend's room, to your RA's room, to the university health services, to the campus police, wherever you need to go to be secure.

Don't be embarrassed about asking the school for help. If your roommate has a serious problem, the sooner they get help, the better (whether or not they realize it at the time— see Chapter 9). And even if they don't have a problem, but things have just gone way wrong between the two of you, talking with your roommate in the presence of a dean, RA, or mediator can help you get back on track.

THE SURPRISING BENEFITS OF GIVING UP

What if nothing helps? After all your efforts, it still feels like you're walking on eggshells, and you're feeling more resentment, not less. Beware of two common reactions that only end up creating more trouble.

The Fixer and the Vengeance Demon

Everyone has tendencies toward being either a fixer or a vengeance demon, and not only can these tendencies hurt your rooming situation, they can wreck your whole year.

Fixers need every relationship to work out. No matter what, their roommate *has* to like them. They're willing to do anything to have a "good" relationship, even if it means making themselves miserable. They'll be extra nice, extra fair, extra friendly, extra whatever-it-takes. And if things don't go well, they'll take all the blame, no matter what's actually causing the problem.

Vengeance demons are the opposite: they're the victim and everything is their roommate's fault. Instead of dealing with the resentment by sticking up for themselves and talking things through, they try to get even. They end up wasting valuable time thinking about how to get back at their roommate, assuming this will make them feel better about their situation—but it doesn't.

Accepting the Limits of Change

It may frustrate you to think that even being super nice won't necessarily make your roommate like you. And you'll have to come to terms with the fact that your roommate is unlikely to suddenly become more ethical, compassionate, and fair-spirited just because you poured maple syrup all over their underwear the night before. Your roommate isn't thinking, "I learned my lesson," they're thinking, "What a jerk."

Changing someone else is a rough business to be in. Accepting the world for what it is is a hard lesson. Once you've done your absolute best to work things through with your roommate, then you're done. We don't literally mean you should give up. We mean you should stop worrying about the situation. Focus on yourself instead. Feel proud of yourself for having had the courage to try to make things better, and then go about the business of having a great year.

2
Social Life

Sweeneee: Just got back from the Omega party!!!

Dunk431: How were the office chair demolition derby and the tapioca slip 'n slide?

Sweeneee: Didn't materialize, but the chicks were hot.

Dunk431: Like how hot?

Sweeneee: On a scale where red is not hot and blue is totally hot, they'd be highly blue.

Dunk431: Shouldn't red be hot? As in "red hot."

Sweeneee: Dude, you're missing the point. It doesn't matter which color is which.

Dunk431: It only matters in the way that making sense versus sounding stupid matters.

Sweeneee: The point is the girls were sexy.

Dunk431: Blue hot!

Sweeneee: Hella blue hot!

Social life can mean a lot different things—dancing at a party in the Quad, bonding with the guys on the lacrosse team, arguing with your roommate about Imperial Rome, or working the night shift at the newspaper.

But whatever being social looks like on the surface, underneath it's all the same: it's about finding connection and community, a place where you feel valued and understood. Social life may be extracurricular, but it's not optional. Finding a place to belong may be the most important thing you can do to feel happy and grounded in college. It's the antidote to homesickness, and the best way to keep the blues at bay.

THE CONVERSATION WITH YOURSELF

Some people are naturally social. They find it easy to start conversations with complete strangers. When in groups, they love telling stories or making jokes, and have a knack for getting the conversational ball rolling. But most people find being in new social situations at least a little bit daunting or uncomfortable, and some find it downright painful.

Why? Is it about how you look or how smart you are? How others treat you and what they think of you? Which parties you go to and how quick you are with an opening line?

Any of these could be factors, but the biggest cause of stress may come as a surprise: it's how you *think*. It's not the conversation you're having with other people; it's the one you're having with yourself. The benefits of changing that conversation are huge. Below, we'll look at some of those conversations and at some of the thinking errors people make. We'll show you how to identify the errors, and how to straighten out your social life by straightening out your thoughts.

AVOID THE INSIDE-OUT TRAP

If you called us up and said, "I don't have time to read your whole book. Just give me the single most helpful piece of advice you've got," our answer would be this: *don't fall into the Inside-Out Trap*. It's the granddaddy of all thinking errors, the one that creates the most unnecessary pain for college students. It has a huge impact on social life, but really it applies to every aspect of college. The good news is that it's not hard to spot and it's something you can change.

The Inside-Out Trap is about how you see yourself in comparison to others.

From: Macani
To: Craig
Sent: Sunday, September 5, 12:18 AM
Subject: me and my shadow

Hey Craig,

Went to the big "dorm meeting" yesterday, where the RA gives you the lowdown on the rules. As I was listening to everyone introduce themselves, it suddenly occurred to me—I'M NOT GOOD AT ANYTHING!! Sewing? Trumpet? Holding my breath? Nothing! Every single other person in the dorm has some amazing talent. Don't believe it? Let's go right down the list. PJ: crew. Lateasha: speaks German. Dave: won a national photography contest. Rollo: computers. Sweeney: hot, popular, has it all. Rajib: student government. Jocie: was on two TV commercials. Johnny: has rich parents.

And me? Oh, I guess I excel at being short and spilling things. No one can take that away from me. And I'm really good at worrying, overanalyzing, and walking into a room and having absolutely no one notice.

Enjoying college,
Macani

There's nothing wrong with comparing yourself to others. We all do it. Like Macani, we want to know whether we're cool, interesting, smart, funny, attractive, and talented. We figure that out by looking around at others and seeing how we stack up. How you rate can have an enormous impact on your self-image and social confidence.

But there's a catch. When comparing ourselves to others, we compare our *insides* to everyone else's *outsides*, and we're left feeling needlessly down and discouraged.

The View from Inside

We all have internal lives that no one else has access to. We have thoughts and feelings and experiences that impact how we see ourselves that we don't often share with others. We're more likely to talk about the successes while keeping the failures, embarrassments, and peculiarities to ourselves. You're more likely to answer the question "How's it going?" by saying, "Pretty good" than by saying, "Well, last night I was lying in bed at three in the morning, consumed with loneliness."

So we're each aware of our own weaknesses and insecurities, yet we rarely have access to those things in other people. When we compare ourselves to others, we notice that no one else seems to have quite as much to feel lousy about as we do. But that's an illusion.

Macani, for example, thinks Sweeney "has it all." That's because she can't see his internal life. Sure, Sweeney is attractive and self-confident, but everyone has their problems in life, and Sweeney is no exception. If Macani had access to Sweeney's internal life, or even to his e-mail, she would hear about his roommate problems, his struggles with academics, and as we'll see later, his battles with his father over how he should handle his future.

The Distortion Is Campuswide

The problem is compounded by the way students are portrayed in the campus media. Brochures and student newspapers feature articles about the sports stars and student geniuses—the senior who is projected to be a third-round pick in the NFL; the freshman who won an international award for her work on the mating rituals of frogs; the junior who spent a summer working for a nonprofit in Honduras.

Missing from the newspaper are stories about people's internal lives—all the things they're thinking and feeling at any given moment. It's not news, of course, but what if it were? Articles about the other students in Macani's dorm might look like this:

The Daily Insider

DAVE FRETS OVER CHEMISTRY QUIZ, PENIS SIZE

"I'm pretty sure I got questions 4 through 10 completely wrong," complained frosh Dave Stukus, who added, "And I'll be darned if I'm not still wondering if my penis is too small."

JOCIE HAS ADMISSIONS NIGHTMARE

"I had this horrible dream last week," confessed Jocie Smith, a first-year student. "The admissions office called to tell me I had been let in by mistake, and the letter of acceptance was actually intended for my dog. They asked me if I wanted to tell everyone about it or whether they should call my friends and family for me. I haven't slept since."

Remember That Everyone Is Struggling with Something

Of course, knowing about the Inside-Out Trap won't stop you from making comparisons, but it will help you put your comparisons into better perspective. Next time you're among other students—whether at a party, in class, or at a meeting of a student organization—pay attention to the information you're using to decide how you stack up. If you can catch yourself before falling into the Inside-Out Trap, it will help you feel more comfortable and confident in social situations.

It's not about reveling in the imagined pain of others. It's about remembering that you're not alone in feeling anxious or insecure and wondering if you're "good enough." Even the students who seem to have everything together struggle with their share of life's challenges. You just can't tell from the outside.

CHALLENGE SUSPECT THOUGHTS

The Inside-Out Trap may be the most significant of the thinking errors, but there are others to watch for as well. Below, we look at three common "suspect thoughts" that relate directly to social life. You'll find yourself having these thoughts on occasion. When you do, our advice is simple: talk back.

Suspect Thought 1: "The Spotlight Is on Me"

In a social situation, it's common to have an exaggerated sense for how aware other people are of you. It's called the spotlight effect. It feels like you're under the glare of a spotlight, and everyone is watching.

From: Sweeney
To: Duncan
Sent: Sunday, September 19, 1:31 PM
Subject: Dining hall

Hey Dunk,

You know what happened to me at dinner? I went through the line with my tray, and I start looking for someone I know to sit with, but come up empty. Did you know that if you stand there long enough with that tray, you eventually trip this alarm and

a voice comes on over the loudspeaker that says, "Alert.
Sweeney is looking for someone to sit with but can't find
anyone. Please stare at him."

I swear, it happened exactly that way, Dunk. Has that ever
happened to you? Or are you too cool?

Sweeney

Everyone goes to the dining hall by themselves occasionally. Some students don't mind it, and even enjoy the time to themselves. Others turn it into a big deal in their minds.

It's not the prospect of eating alone that bothers Sweeney. It's his concern about what everyone might be thinking. The spotlight is trained on him, and he feels like an Olympic skater who keeps tripping during his performance.

Talking back to your thoughts means recognizing that everyone *isn't* looking at you. Most people are too busy worrying about themselves to be paying much attention to how long it takes you to find someone to sit with. They think the spotlight is on them, so obviously it can't be on you.

What does it say about you to be eating by yourself? Not much. In fact, going to the dining hall on your own is actually a good way to meet new people. It's worth trying, even if it's out of your comfort zone. Look for someone else who is sitting alone, or look for someone you've met before but don't know well. Then it's just a matter of saying, "Hey, mind if I join you? Aren't you in my economics class?" or, "Is anyone sitting here?"

Suspect Thought 2:
"Everyone at This Party Knows Each Other"

Like Rollo, you've probably been to parties where you felt out of place. Whether it's at a mixer or at the initial meeting of an organization, when you feel out of place, it seems like everyone else is "in place." All the other people at the party seem to know each other. In fact, you assume they're all best friends and that they're all having the time of their lives.

But it's just not true.

The real story is more complicated. Some people are doing well, others are feeling at least as uncomfortable as you, and in any event, the whole thing is a lot more complicated than you imagine. A drawing that better captures the actual party dynamic might look like this:

Challenging the assumption that everyone else is "in place" and you're the odd person out can help you to feel more comfortable at the party. In any case, the goal is to have fun and meet people, and you can't do that if you leave the party at the first moment you feel tense. Going home and playing video games or getting under the covers may feel soothing, but it won't do much for your social life.

The forty-five-minute rule. If you tend to leave parties, study breaks, or other social gatherings early, go with a friend and agree in advance that no matter how bored or awkward you feel, you'll stay for at least forty-five minutes. This gets exponentially harder when the friend you've gone with suddenly meets someone, and now you're totally on your own. This would be an easy excuse to leave, but don't. Stay the full forty-five minutes. You might meet someone five minutes after your friend does or you might not. Over time, your chances of having an interesting conversation or even meeting someone you like go way up if you hang in there.

Suspect Thought 3:
"I'm Alone, So I'm a Loser"

On occasion, you're going to feel lonely in college. It's a pretty safe bet. Such feelings can be particularly intense during the first few weeks or months of school. Longing to be with others at school is all mixed up with longing to be with your old friends from home. Of course, even after you've found a community that is right for you, there will still be lonely times.

Loneliness seems to be an emotion that is built into the human soul.

To: Merriam-Webster Dictionary
From: Rollo
Sent: Friday, October 8, 11:05 PM
Subject: def. "lonely"

Dear Merriam,

I am writing to petition for a definition change for the word "lonely." The current definition is "sad from being alone," but my loneliest moments occur at parties and other social gatherings. Please adjust your definition as appropriate, and feel free to use me as a reference.

Best wishes,
Rollo (noun)

As Rollo points out, "loneliness" and "being alone" are two different things. Being alone is just a description of how many people you're with (none). Loneliness, in contrast, is an *emotion* (part sadness, part longing). You can feel lonely in a crowd or perfectly content on your own.

The intensity of the loneliness you feel is based in part on the *meaning* you give to the situation. If being by yourself means "I'm alone, so I'm a loser," you'll feel a whole lot worse than if being by yourself means "I'm normal; like everyone else, I'm struggling to find people I like and a place to fit in."

When you do find yourself alone, take a look at the story you're telling yourself about why you're alone and what it means. If you're beating yourself up for being by yourself or for failing to meet someone at a party, that's when it's time to talk back.

Loneliness: Saturday night and you're all alone. Why aren't you at that party with Macani?

PJ: Uh, I don't know. She didn't invite me.

Loneliness: I see. That's the first sign.

PJ: What are you talking about?

Loneliness: That she doesn't like you. This is all starting to make sense.

PJ: What?

Loneliness: She's just pretending to like you because she can't escape from living with you. You know, making the best of a bad situation.

PJ: Hey, I'm trying to watch a movie here.

Loneliness: Someone's rude. No wonder you don't have any friends. Oh, by the way, where are all the girls from the crew team?

PJ: Hmm. Good question. I don't know.

Loneliness: They're probably off doing something fun without you. I guess the whole "having friends on the crew team" thing isn't quite working out.

PJ: Just because I'm spending a Saturday night by myself doesn't mean I'm not going to have friends on the team. These things take time.

Loneliness: If it makes you feel better to think that, then go ahead.

PJ: Okay, fine, next weekend I'll try harder to find something social to do. But right now, I just want to watch this movie. Popcorn?

PJ does a nice job of bringing some perspective to being alone. She's not denying that she feels lonely, but she's not making the mistake of thinking it's the end of the world.

TWO MYTHS ABOUT FRIENDSHIP

Whether you're going to college with a couple of friends from high school or heading off to a college where you don't know a soul, making new friends is important. Some students moved a lot when they were growing up and are used to the various ups and downs that go along with making friends. For others, college may literally be the first time since grade school that they've had to give the matter any thought.

Even the phrase *making friends* has a grammar school ring to it. But that doesn't mean we somehow master the art by a certain age. Making friends is something you do over a lifetime, and even people who are good at it tend to buy into certain myths about how it happens and what it means.

The Instant Friendship Myth

From: Macani
To: Craig
Sent: Monday, September 6, 3:10 PM
Subject: friends

Okay, Craig, this whole thing about going to college and making lifelong friends is crap. I've been here for six entire days and I haven't made a single lifelong friend. I guess there's always tomorrow, but I'm getting tired of waiting.

Macani

You'll meet hundreds of people during that first rush of campus events, and you may or may not make a good friend at the outset. But be patient. You'll continue to meet people during the rest of the year and, in fact, during all four years of school. Some of the best friendships take time to unfold.

It's often hard to tell who you'll end up getting along with. It's not always the person you like the most when you first meet. The arrogant guy who crushed you in basketball when you played one-on-one the first week of school could end up being your best friend on the intramural team. Your boss at the library? A friendship seemed pretty unlikely with her, yet there it is. So keep an open mind about who fits into the "potential friend" category.

Students with really close friends from high school run a particularly high risk of being closed-minded about new people they meet.

Instant Messenger

Sweeneee: Dude, why didn't we go to college together?
Dunk431: I don't know. That woulda been sweet.
Sweeneee: The people here have no sense of humor—they don't even get my pirate joke.

Dunk431: How can they not get your pirate joke??? It makes life
worth living!!!

Sweeneee: That's what I'm saying. It's a complete wasteland.

If you are lucky enough to have good friends from high school, that's a good thing. The mistake students make is to compare the new people they're meeting at school against their longtime friends from home. Of course these new acquaintances don't "get you" as well as your old friends do. But your old friends didn't "get you" at first, either. It's important to invest in your friendships from high school, but if you find that they're the only people you call or e-mail, then it's time to make an adjustment. Don't use the availability of old friends as a way to avoid the work involved in making new ones.

The Popularity Myth

It's a mistake to assume that the person who is the life of the party is always the best at making and keeping good friends. Ease in groups requires a different set of skills from being able to establish deep and enduring friendships.

Think about what you like about your friends. It's probably not the traits we typically associate with being popular, like being the best looking, the best athlete, or the most outgoing. Your friends may be any of those things, but that's not what you enjoy about their company. They're great to hang out with because you have common interests and a similar sense of humor, and you trust them enough that you can relax and be yourself. Being popular is optional; having meaningful friendships isn't.

ACTIVITIES AND ORGANIZATIONS

When it comes to extracurriculars, there are plenty of options. Student groups provide much of the richness of campus life, and it's a huge mistake not to take advantage of what they have to offer.

From: Macani
To: Craig
Sent: Tuesday, September 14, 9:12 PM
Subject: Signed up

Hey Craig:

Remember that singing group I tried out for, the High Doodlies? Well, I got "Hi Don't-ed." Jerks.

But it's okay, there are plenty of other options out there—Arts for Tots, the Poetry Journal, the Campus Recyling Outreach, the Women's Center, the Young Accountants Association, the Monthly Nut Humor Magazine, the Jewish-Islamic discussion group, and something called the Young Teamsters Union. And, of course, there's still the drama society callbacks.

I think I'll join whichever group hates the High Doodlies the most. . . . Ideally, that would be a group called Students Against High Doodlies.

Macani

Richard Light, a professor at Harvard, studied how extracurriculars affect student happiness and academic performance. He found that students who participated in extracurricular activities were more satisfied with their college experience than those who didn't. That's no surprise; many of your fondest high school memories probably involve extracurriculars.

More surprising is that Professor Light found that many students said they learned more from their extracurricular activities than from their classes. It makes sense. If you're involved in a project that helps young schoolchildren design murals in their neighborhoods, imagine what you'd learn about child psychology, art, city planning, and the very practical skill of making things happen. Imagine the relationships you might develop and the sense of accomplishment you'd get from seeing the mural completed, overcoming all the barriers along the way.

Despite the importance of extracurricular activities, some students don't participate. Why? A few concerns stand out.

"I Have No Time"

Professor Light to the rescue. His study found that, with the exception of varsity athletes, students who participate in one or two major extracurricular activities get the same grades as students who don't. So there's plenty of time to get involved, no matter how heavy your academic load. On average, varsity athletes' grades did suffer slightly; on the other hand, these same athletes said that their participation in sports made their college experience significantly more fulfilling.

"I'm Not Good Enough at Anything"

Wrong. You may not be good enough to be the starting defensive end on the football team or managing editor of the literary journal, but everyone is good enough to participate in something meaningful in college.

For many activities, nothing is required other than a commitment to working hard. If you don't have writing talent to bring to a paper or journal, you might be able to participate on the business end, selling advertisements. If you don't have the voice for radio, you might be able to work behind the scenes. If you don't have any acting ability, you might find a niche in set design or lighting.

One of the best things you can do for an organization is to "hang around and help." It may not sound glamorous, but that's how a lot of people who end up with interesting jobs in organizations get their start. If you're willing to do the dirty work as a first- or second-year student, your commitment will usually be rewarded. A surprising amount of being really good at something comes from just having been around while things were happening and paying attention. If you're not willing to start at the bottom, you may never get started at all.

Finally, don't shun an organization just because "anyone can join." It's true that anyone can join a social outreach program, for example. If you can read, they'll let you tutor a child in reading. But not everyone will be good at it, and not everyone will have the perseverance to continue the work even when it's inconvenient or frustrating. The bigger point is this: whether or not an organization is exclusive doesn't determine its value to you or to society.

"It Wasn't Fun"

This concern brings us back to being willing to start at the bottom. Finding a place to belong doesn't mean finding a place where everything is absolutely perfect, where everyone loves you 24/7, and where you get to do exactly what you want when you want.

It takes time. It takes time to get to know other students. It takes time for them to get to know and value you. It takes time to get good enough at what you're doing so that it starts to feel enjoyable. It takes time to make a difference in the world. If you don't like an activity after two weeks, give it more time. If you find something in the meantime that seems to fit you better, then by all means make the jump. But don't keep joining and quitting. It's like going swimming in the ocean. When you first jump in, it feels impossibly cold and unpleasant. But if you don't stick it out, you'll never get to the rewards that lie on the other side of the pain.

DEALING WITH GROUP ENVY

Being accepted by a group of people you admire feels great. The group can be anything: kids who went to a certain prep school; the gang of "funny guys" who sit together in the cafeteria; computer geniuses; the executive board of the Latino Students Association.

And being rejected—whether formally by an organization or a fraternity, or informally by a group of students who don't seem to want to hang out with you—feels like crap.

From: Rollo
To: Chess Team
Sent: Tuesday, October 5, 6:15 PM
Subject: error

Dear Team,

I discovered a serious error on the chess team roster, which was posted online two and a half minutes ago. Your list appears to have been entered in reverse order, as my name was placed at the bottom of the alternates list rather than at the top of the roster.

As you no doubt know from reading my admissions essay, the chess team was the only reason I came to this institution in the first place.

I love you guys. How could you do this to me???

Rollo

We'll talk in more detail about how to deal with failure or rejection in the chapters on Academics and Relationships. For now, what matters is this: it's okay to feel hurt; it's okay to feel envious; it's okay to feel longing. But if you aren't accepted into one group, it's crucial to find another group to join. It may not feel as fulfilling at first, but the energy you put into whatever you choose to do will gather meaning over time. Make sure your college years are defined by what you did do, not by what you didn't.

FRATERNITIES AND SORORITIES

There are few topics regarding campus life that people feel as strongly about or are as divided over as fraternities and sororities. For some, frats and sororities are the single most important aspect of their college life. The people in the house are not just friends, but family (hence, "brother" and "sister"), and the bonds last a lifetime.

These associations provide firsthand experience in balancing freedom and responsibility. Members are often in charge of a house, including everything from cooking and cleaning, to making decisions about when to paint the exterior and whether to spend money upgrading the plumbing. Most frats and sororities are also involved in volunteer work to improve the campus or local community.

Others hold a different view of frats and sororities. They worry about the perpetuation of outdated or even dangerous attitudes about men, women, and sex, and they are concerned about a culture that can promote excessive drinking. Increasingly, the organizations are aware of the importance of these issues and are working hard at improving the culture while maintaining what is unique about them.

In this regard, it's crucial to remember that fraternities and sororities are responsible to the college and the community at large, even though they can seem like worlds unto themselves. Students are required to follow university rules and applicable laws about hazing (i.e., it's prohibited and illegal), as well as laws relating to underage drinking, drugs, sexual assault, and rape. Don't assume that just because something takes place in a frat house or sorority, there won't be consequences.

If you join a house, it's *your* organization. There can be substantial differences from house to house, so find one that fits you best, and work hard to keep it a place you're proud of.

DRINKING AND DRUGS

The problem with some of the sermonizing about alcohol or drugs is that it's not honest. Drinking = bad. End of story.

But let's face it: people drink for a reason. It can create a sense of euphoria and confidence. The music's blasting, the lights are flashing, and you're out on the dance floor. You're seriously buzzed and having the time of your life. "Check out these dance moves!" "I'm the funniest guy on the planet!" "This is the greatest party there's ever been!" "Hi, I'm Harold! Chicks love me!"

Sure, drinking and using drugs can seem like good ways to relieve the stress of college life. But life is not a beer commercial. In the real world, actions have consequences. When you drink to excess or take drugs, you can end up getting into real trouble or putting yourself or others in danger.

From: Sweeney
To: Duncan
Sent: Saturday, December 4, 3:47 AM
Subject: chunks

Hey Dunk,

Horrible night. Me, Cube, José, and Oak go drinking with the Sigma guys, and Oak tries to impress them with how much he can drink, and he's just getting shit-faced, and everyone's on the floor laughing, and then he gets really sick. Like incoherent and puking. So we call Security, and they're only allowed to take him to health services in an ambulance, which was scary as hell. He's okay now, but what happened was not cool. And now Oak's all, "Yeah, let's get wasted next weekend!" What the fuck???

Sweeney

Sweeney and his friends were right to seek medical help, and likely avoided a much more serious situation by doing so. But it's also worth considering the choices leading up to Oak's getting sick: whether Sweeney and his friends should have allowed (or even encouraged) Oak to drink as much as he did; whether Oak should have been more watchful of his own limits; whether he should even drink at all if he knows he will lose control.

Alcohol is a big deal. If you want to drink, you have a duty to yourself and those around you to consider the choices and consequences involved.

It's Against the Law

First things first: drug possession is illegal. Buying alcohol if you're under the age of twenty-one (or supplying it to those who are underage) is illegal. Your school might have additional penalties for students caught on campus with drugs or alcohol; these can range from admonishment to expulsion.

Regardless of whether you think "everyone is doing it," you're still responsible if you get caught.

Can You Drink Responsibly?

The wisest thing is to avoid alcohol altogether.

But if you are going to drink, drink responsibly. That means limiting yourself to a couple of drinks and being aware of your own tendencies when you drink. It means going to parties with friends and making sure you don't let each other go off alone with someone when one or both of the people involved has been drinking. It means making sure your friends get home safely.

And if you've never had a drink before, don't drink for the first time at a big party full of other people who are drinking. You don't know how you'll react to alcohol.

Drinking responsibly may be tougher than it sounds. The problem is that the one or two drinks you start with can actually cause you to change your mind about how much you're going to drink. Once you've had one drink, it's easy to think, "What the hell, I'll have a couple more." And a couple more. And before you know it, you're in deep waters.

Four Really Stupid Thoughts

There are endless ways drinking or taking drugs can get you in trouble, but four are worth particular mention. If you find yourself thinking any of the following, think again.

"We're drunk. Let's have sex now and figure things out later." Figure what out later? Whether there's mutual consent? Whether to use birth control? When you're drunk, you're not in a state of mind to make any of the important decisions involved in sex. Alcohol can lead to aggressive behavior and, at the same time, an indifference to consequences. That's a recipe for disaster. Alcohol and drugs play a role in a substantial percentage of rapes and sexual assaults on college campuses. There's more on this in Chapter 7.

"I'm a good drunk driver." If you have this thought, it may be the most dangerous (and dumbest) thought you'll ever have in your life. There's no such thing as a good drunk driver. Period. And if you're thinking, "Well, it's not very far" or, "I'm not really *that* drunk" or, "I'm not sure how else to get home so I have to drive," this is your brain telling you not to. If you're trying to calculate whether or not you're legally intoxicated, you're already way over the line.

The only responsible way to handle things is to make plans *in advance* for how to get where you need to go after a party where alcohol is served.

From: Rollo
To: Amy
Sent: Saturday, November 6, 5:45 PM
Subject: oh me

Dear Amy,

It's me, Rollo, the guy on the first floor. I just got back from the football game, and I was wedged in between two alumni who were passing a flask back and forth, and each time they passed it to me, I took a swig just like they did, and this is the first time I've ever had a drink with alcohol in it, and a lot of

Social Life ■ 47

them I might add. Maybe I just don't get drunk very easily, but I don't think the alcohol has had any effect on me or my personality.

Rollo

P.S. I know we don't really know each other, but I think I'm in love with you. What might the next step be?

"It wasn't the real me." Yes, it was.

The sober version of yourself has judgment. It recognizes that propositioning the guy or girl upstairs who you don't really know is probably not the best idea. But the alcohol wrestles your judgment into submission. Suddenly, breaking the windows of your chemistry lab, taking a swing at a cop, or taking a piss on your couch (to put out the fire you set) can seem like a great idea.

Afterward, you might think, "Well, gee, that's not how I normally act. Everyone knows that's not the real me." But it is the real you. It's always you, and you're responsible for your actions. When you choose to drink, you're also choosing to accept the consequences.

"Puking or not, I've got to win this drinking game." There are all sorts of social pressures to drink more than you would ordinarily choose, whether it's a drinking game, a birthday party where friends keep buying you drinks, or simply an attempt to keep up with how much others seem to be drinking. In the moment, your own level of intoxication takes a backseat to the social goal at stake.

Sure, having people like you is important. Having fun is important. But if you think people won't like you because you stopped drinking before you got sick, that's just stupid. Trust us—if people like you, it's in spite of your ability to win at beer pong, not because of it. They don't want to clean the vomit off the floor tomorrow morning any more than you do.

Regardless of the game, don't urge someone else to keep drinking past a moderate amount. Cheering other people on stops being fun when you have to stay up all night taking care of a drunk friend, or when someone needs to be rushed to the emergency room with alcohol poisoning.

Consider these statistics: it is estimated that 1,100 college students die every year from drinking and driving, approximately 400 students die each year from non-driving-related alcohol deaths, and another 500,000 become injured or ill. More than 1 percent of college students attempt suicide because of alcohol or drug use. And students who abuse alcohol are twenty-one times more likely to miss class, fall behind in school, damage property, or get into trouble with campus police.*

*These statistics come from the National Institute on Alcohol Abuse and Alcoholism, and from the Harvard School of Public Health's College Alcohol Study.

GUIDELINES FOR HELPING A FRIEND WHO IS DRUNK

At colleges with high drinking rates, 57 percent of students reported that they've taken care of an intoxicated friend. If you were to find yourself in that situation, would you know what to do? The following information comes from Harvard University's Health Services Web site°:

You can't sober them up: Coffee, water, cold showers, or exercise cannot speed up the sobering up process. Your liver can only metabolize about one ounce of alcohol per hour. (One ounce is about the amount found in one can of beer, one glass of wine, or one mixed drink or "shot.")

If your friend is unconscious: A person who has passed out, or is asleep and cannot be awakened or can only be aroused for a few moments, needs urgent care. **Do not** assume he or she is "just sleeping it off." People who have made this assumption later discovered (too late) that the friend was in a fatal coma. When in doubt, check for these signs: breathing is very slow and perhaps irregular; pulse is weak, or is either very slow or very fast; hands or feet are colder than normal.

If your friend is conscious:

Never leave the drunk person alone. The full effects may not yet have kicked in.

Keep the drunk person from driving, biking, or going anywhere alone.

Turn the drunk person on his or her side or stomach to prevent aspiration of vomit (inhaling own vomit).

Don't give the person any drugs or medication (not even aspirin!) to try to sober him or her up.

Coffee, tea, and other caffeinated beverages won't help. You'll only end up with a wide-awake, agitated drunk person.

°See http://www.huhs.harvard.edu/HealthInformation.

You can't prevent the alcohol from being absorbed once it has been consumed. Giving the drunk person food will increase the risk of vomiting.

Skip the folk remedies. A cold shower could make the drunk person pass out or fall. Exercise won't help and could cause an injury.

If your friend argues with you, don't take what is said personally.

Talk to your friend about his or her behavior *later on*, in a private place.

If your friend becomes agitated or violent: Keep your distance and get help. Some people who are usually very gentle-natured can become violent when intoxicated.

Having a social life is important. If your social life is going to involve alcohol, please remember that the real world doesn't stop the moment you take a drink. You still have to follow the law, and you still have a moral obligation to take care of yourself and those around you.

3
Academics

Hey Craig:

So we're reading *A Streetcar Named Desire* in my American theater class, and the professor who is like a hundred years old starts telling us about how he was friends with Tennessee Williams!! And times when they went out drinking together, and all these things "Tennessee" said. The whole class is only 22 students, and I'm just sitting there 5 feet from the guy and it was so amazing. I LOVE this class (I don't know how to make a heart on my computer).

Macani

Some college courses are inspiring, others less so. Like Macani, Rollo likes his classes, although he is not without the occasional complaint.

From: Rollo
To: Guinness Book of World Records
Sent: Tuesday, September 14, 3:27 PM
Subject: My economics class

To whom it may concern:

I would like to register a world record. My Introduction to Microeconomics class has 37,409 students in it. I think a professor teaches it, but I'm not certain since I sit too far away to see.

Rollo

All classes, whether they're thrilling or dull, hard or easy, have a few things in common: grades, workload, professors, and the not so small matter of learning something. Figuring out how to navigate these issues isn't always easy.

WHAT'S IN A GRADE?

Grades are not unlike Homer Simpson's characterization of alcohol: "the cause of and solution to all life's problems." It's easy to fantasize about the promise of good grades: the doors of opportunity that fly open at the sight of your golden transcript; the Teflon armor of intellectual achievement; the absence of harassing phone calls from parents.

At the same time, grades are like lighter fluid for the smoldering embers of anxiety: What if I turn out not to be one of the "smart" students? Or, what if it turns out that I can't succeed at college-level work?

And what will grades mean for my future? What if I don't get into medical school or a decent law school? What if a potential employer wants to see my transcript? What if I have no idea what I want to do, but in some theoretical future my grades prevent me from doing precisely that? These are all fair questions to be asking, so let's take a look.

GRADES AND SELF-IMAGE

From: PJ
To: Macani
Sent: Friday, November 5, 11:14 AM
Subject: poli sci grade

Hey Macani,

I just got my midterm back in poli sci. "B minus." I guess the good news is that I'm officially smart enough for college. So in a way I'm relieved, but in a way I'm disappointed. In high school, I wasn't the smartest one but I did well by working really hard, just like in crew. Maybe that doesn't work in college. How hard can they expect me to study? I'm feeling sort of jealous of the people who got A's on this test.

> I feel like I'm being left out of something, and I don't even
> know what.
>
> PJ

Grades have the power to shape, and in some cases puncture, your self-image. College, the thinking goes, may reveal you to be a true genius—or not so bright after all. Either way, it will be your grades that tell. Or so many students think.

Am I Smart?

It's true that people who get good grades are usually pretty smart. But being smart doesn't guarantee good grades in college, and getting poor or average grades doesn't mean you aren't smart. A number of factors unrelated to intelligence (however you want to define that word) will impact your grades.

Course selection and placement issues. Nothing will mess you up quicker than taking courses for which you don't have the appropriate background. If a placement exam says you should take an intro-level course, you had better have an awfully good reason for thinking you belong in a more advanced course. Too often students sign up for a more advanced course because they were "advanced" in high school, or to prove to themselves how smart they are, or to impress some imaginary graduate school admissions officer, or because they're in some sort of hurry. Or maybe they're simply positive they can do the work, and they want to free up an extra elective down the road.

None of these is a good reason for jumping ahead. Your

only concern should be taking the level that is appropriate for you based on your background and skill. Take your placement test results and conversations with advisors *very* seriously.

The same is true for loading up on difficult courses (even if the placement is right), or taking more courses than the standard number. College courses are harder than high school courses. They're more work and require more thought. Science courses go faster and deeper. Courses in the liberal arts and social sciences involve significantly more reading and writing.

Once you have a successful semester or two under your belt, you can make an informed choice about taking five classes instead of the recommended four (rarely a good idea in any event), or three hard courses in the same semester, instead of one or two. But don't get overloaded on hard courses your very first semester. You're flying blind, and the potential downside is too great.

Class size. Surprisingly, the size of your classes can also impact grades. Students who take only large lecture courses in their freshman year are a little more likely to struggle than those who take at least one smaller class.* It's not clear why the correlation exists, but you can imagine that students who take at least one small class are more likely to have a sense of connection—to their classmates, to the professor, to the subject matter. The more connected you feel, the more interesting things will be, and the more likely you are to feel motivated to study. So, no matter what sort of requirements you face, take at least one small class during your first semester.

The professor's expectations. Grades are also based in part on how well your work in each class conforms to the pro-

---

*Richard Light, *Making the Most of College* (Cambridge, Mass.: Harvard University Press, 2001).

fessor's expectations. Not expectations as in "high standards," but rather how the professor expects things to be done—how papers should be organized, how to write a test, how labs should be handled. These are all things you can't know when you first arrive on campus, but can learn over time, either through experience, by talking with upperclassmen, or by talking directly with your instructors.

The role of studying. Probably the biggest factor in how well you do in college is how hard and how smart you study. That's lucky because it's something you have control over. We'll talk more about study habits in Chapter 4; the point here is that grades are a reflection of many factors in addition to just "being smart."

GRADES AND YOUR FUTURE

If you look at a list of people who graduated from your college with the highest grade point average for each year since the school was founded, you'll notice something striking: most likely, you will not have heard of a single one. That's not a comment on your particular college. It's true of every college.

Why? A big reason is that grades and book learning alone don't determine success in life. Qualities like creativity, passion, resourcefulness, courage, empathy, humor, optimism, and persistence are what make the Nelson Mandelas, Steven Spielbergs, and Jane Goodalls of the world. Yes, the learning and thinking skills you acquire in college are crucial, but so are many other talents that aren't measured by a grade.

Even so, it is true that in many arenas, grades matter. In law, medicine, business, and other fields of graduate studies, grades are a big factor in how candidates are evaluated. And many employers are looking for graduates who have excelled academically, either generally or in particular classes related to the area of employment.

The bottom line? In some contexts, grades make a difference; in others, less so. Ultimately, you should keep in mind the difference between what you can control and what you can't. You can't control whether you were born with an affinity for mathematical problem solving or a gift for language. You can't control whether a particular professor appreciates your writing style or sense of humor. You can't control whether you get sick on the day of the final.

But there are some things you can control. Choose courses wisely. Learn as much as you can about what a particular instructor is looking for and how he or she evaluates you. And most important of all, study hard and study smart.

RESILIENCE AND THE ART OF LEARNING FROM DISAPPOINTMENT

Of course, no matter how much effort you put in, it's simply not possible to get through college without encountering failure. Setbacks may come in the form of disappointing grades, being rejected for an honors major, or being informed by a professor that she's chosen someone else to work with her in the lab. College can also bring personal setbacks—getting cut from a team, being turned down for a date. Every college student, somewhere along the road to graduation, encounters something that tests his or her ability to handle failure.

The best way to handle failure is to learn from it. Everyone knows that. The more interesting question is, why are some people so amazingly good at taking setbacks in stride, while others have a harder time getting back on their feet? A few factors help explain the difference.

Am I a Failure, or Did I Fail?

When things don't go your way, what does it say about you? Your answer to the question has a big impact on how you deal with failure.

Some people let a failure define their identity: "I failed, therefore, *I'm* a failure." "I didn't just *get* a D minus, *I am* a D minus. I'm stupid, unworthy . . ." and so forth. It's easy to imagine how this might affect your motivation. If you're a failure, why bother doing anything? It's just another opportunity to realize how much you suck.

Others see things differently: "I failed. I'm the sort of person who tries things, fails, and then tries again." Their identity is defined not by the failure but by their resilience in the face of failure. Because so many tasks in life involve repeated setbacks before effort is rewarded—doing research, improving your writing skills, finding romance—it's easy to see why resilience matters.

We're not saying that you shouldn't feel bad when things don't work out. The things you are trying to accomplish in college take a lot of work, and they're important to you. Feeling rejected, disappointed, and anxious are appropriate responses to the situation. It means you understand what's going on.

At the same time, you have some choice in how you *think* about what has happened. There is a world of difference between asking yourself, "What have I learned and how can I improve?" versus asking, "What's wrong with me? Why am I such a loser?" And that difference can have a big impact on your ability to bounce back.

In thinking about grades, remember that they give you information about your knowledge of a subject, whether you're studying in the right way, and so forth. But there's also something else being "graded" during college, and that is your ability to handle setbacks and to make something productive out of them. Even if you get a D on a Spanish exam, you can still get an A on the resilience exam.

That "invisible grade," believe it or not, is at least as important to your life success as your grade in Spanish. Why? Because you're going to have plenty of setbacks in life, and how you manage them is a big part of the story of whether you feel happy, satisfied, and successful. Resilience is a comparatively rare quality, and it is much cherished and rewarded—in college and in the real world.

My Future: Now on DVD

How well you manage setbacks is also tied to what you think the setback means for your future. Too often, we turn the setback into a catastrophic prediction about our future, a future filled with torment, failure, and despair.

From: Rollo
To: Professor Tran, PhD
Sent: Tuesday, October 5, 5:45 PM
Subject: Quizzical

Hi again,

As you are no doubt aware, I received a grade of C on last week's economics quiz. I am embarrassed to report that I was rather hoping for an A+, with a shot at being known departmentally as "wonder boy." But I'm guessing that's unlikely now, as is my eventual acceptance into graduate school.

I was wondering if you would be so kind as to forward me the names of three other students in our section who received a C or worse. I think it will be helpful for me to discuss certain issues with my new peers, including whether to join the merchant marines, ideas for future low-income housing, and various recipes for making dog food taste just like chicken (I think the trick is to get the chicken-flavored dog food, but I need to consult).

I appreciate your time. My best to Onyi, who is an excellent TA, and if she is beating herself up for my failure to learn, she should not.

Rollo

In his e-mail, Rollo takes what he regards as bad news and spins it forward into the future, making ever more dire predictions about what sort of life awaits him. The thinking goes like this:

I got a disappointing grade = I'll never amount to anything in life.

My boyfriend broke up with me = No one will ever like me.

I got rejected from the frat I liked = I'll never fit in anywhere.

It's raining outside = It will rain forever.

It's a common tendency. When you're upset, the future rarely looks good, and this leads to a downward spiral. If you think your future will be bleak, it makes you feel worse *right now*, which in turn makes the future look even more bleak, which makes you feel even more horrible *right now*. Before you know it, you've got a DVD playing in your head called "My Future: A Descent into Hell."

Getting a disappointing grade is not meaningless, nor is losing a boyfriend or being rejected by an organization you wanted to be a part of. If you get cut from the basketball team as a freshman, it means you won't be on the basketball team as a freshman. It may mean you'll never be on the team. But it says hardly anything about how happy you'll be in college, and nothing about what sort of life you'll lead.

To break the cycle of pessimism, you have to change the DVD. Press Eject, get that crazy DVD out of your head, and put in something more realistic: "This Disappointment: A Balanced View." If you're able to keep perspective on the relationship between a current setback and how you'll really feel in the future, rebounding from disappointment is far easier.

Am I Blaming Everyone Else?

Finally, don't be the type who sees whatever happens to you as totally out of your control. Don't assume bad things are always someone else's fault.

Of course, failures are *related* to what other people do. You're not the one who cut you from the team. You're not the one who broke up with you. You're not the one who gave you an F. So, sure, other people have an impact on your life—but so do you. Your professor graded your paper, but you wrote it. Your coach cut you, but you didn't work out your hardest over the summer. Your girlfriend broke up with you, but you wouldn't stop flirting with other women in front of her.

Not blaming others for things that happen to you means you have to take some responsibility for your own life. That's not always easy, but the more you see yourself as responsible for what happens to you, the more power you have to change the way things turn out next time.

TALKING WITH PROFESSORS, IN CLASS AND AFTER

"What?! You can *talk* to a professor?" Yes. Just like you, professors know words.

Some students feel comfortable approaching a professor with a comment or question; others find the idea ridiculously intimidating. To some extent, it depends on the professor. Do they have an air of "Don't bother me, kid, I'm busy winning the Nobel Prize"? Or do they seem relaxed and inviting?

Your own assumptions about your professors also play a part in how comfortable you feel. Regardless of your professor's attitude, you aren't "in the way." You're the professor's student. You pay the professor's salary. You aren't some sideshow or crazy relative who showed up to a wedding as an uninvited guest. Helping you learn is an important part of a professor's job. They know it, the school knows it, your parents know it—and you should know it too.

Talking in Class

Unless one of your professors is really cool and shows up to your dorm's study breaks, most of your interactions with the faculty will be either in class or at office hours.

Though classes vary in size, you'll have opportunities to talk in class one way or another. That doesn't mean you should raise your hand in the middle of a huge lecture hall and say, "I wasn't listening. Could you start your lecture over?" Your larger classes will usually have smaller "sections" or labs where real conversations about the material can take place.

Talking in front of others is a useful skill in life that gets easier with practice. Most students find it at least a little scary the first few times they talk in class, but it's important to get over that hurdle.

Thinking about the situation from the professor's point of view can help. You might assume your professors' job is to sit back and judge students, but they see their roles quite differently. Professors want the discussion to be lively and provocative, and they almost always appreciate students who try to add something. Sure, professors care about the quality of the comments, but judging you, per se, is not high on their priority list.

To give you some insight into how a class discussion looks from the professor's point of view, we've included a Professor Translator. Here's how it works. Imagine that Macani raises her hand during a class discussion about imperialism and says, "I thought the reading made a good point about how Britain's own economic problems fueled colonial expansion."

Below are three possible responses to Macani's comment, how Macani took the responses, and what the professor may have actually meant:

PROFESSOR SAYS . . .	MACANI HEARS . . .	PROFESSOR MEANT . . .
"Why?"	"He hates my comment. He knows I don't know what I'm talking about and wants to skewer me in front of the class. I should never have opened my mouth . . ."	"Interesting. I'd like to hear more." "Finally, a student willing to made an argument." "I agree with this comment. I'd like the student to elaborate so I don't have to. The students hear enough of my yammering."
"Interesting. Let's put that comment on hold and get back to it."	"My comment is either irrelevant or so stupid that the professor doesn't want to subject me to further embarrassment by allowing me to talk. Now everyone knows how much of a shame it is to have me in this class."	"Uh-oh. This student is raising what we're supposed to cover next week. Quickly, must . . . distract . . . class." "Oh crap, I wasn't listening. I'll tell the class we'll come back to it and hope they forget."

PROFESSOR SAYS . . .	MACANI HEARS . . .	PROFESSOR MEANT . . .
\<silence\>	"Hello? Did he hear what I said? Maybe he's giving me the silent treatment. I want to transfer to an easier college where professors are allowed to actually talk to you."	"Well put." "If I don't jump in, maybe students will begin to respond to each other, which would be nice." "Well, we've covered everything I planned for this class. I need to figure out what to do for the next 45 minutes."

Notice the gap between Macani's reaction and what the professor is actually thinking. Macani thinks it's all about whether or not her comment was good, while the professor is focused on other things.

If you find yourself feeling hesitant to talk in class, here are a few things to keep in mind:

No one knows everything. You emerge from your poli sci class thinking every one else is smarter than you. Why? Because you sat there for the whole hour and noticed how smart the comments were. Sure, you made one good comment, but there were so many others. Here, you're making the classic mistake of adding up all the smart comments and assuming that *each* of the other students could have made *all of them*. Not true. Each student might have had one or two interesting thoughts, but, hey, so did you.

Focus on content. Don't let too much of your attention be taken up with "What do people think of me?" and "What do I think of them?" Instead, keep your mind on the ideas. Really listen to what others are saying, and try to understand them from their point of view. Consider their reasoning and what they may be leaving out. Ask yourself why your interpretation is different. Is it a matter of different values, different experiences, different assumptions? How would you build on their ideas?

Prepare. If you find talking in class particularly stressful, consider jotting down a few thoughts before class. You might also talk with your professor during office hours about how you feel, saying something like, "I get really nervous in class, but I want to try to get over it. I wanted to let you know in advance that I'm going to make a comment today." Most professors will appreciate your effort.

Jump in. Some students don't speak up in class because they can't find a good place to enter the conversation. If you tend to be a polite person and are waiting for a quiet moment before you talk, you could be waiting a long time. Don't be rude, but be assertive. If the norm of the class is to raise your hand, then raise your hand; if the norm of the class is to just jump in, then practice jumping in, even if it feels a little awkward at first. If you aren't sure what the rules of the game are for participation, ask your TA or professor after class.

Getting to Know a Professor

From: Rollo
To: Professor Young
Sent: Wednesday, September 15, 6:24 PM
Subject: student

Dear Professor Young,

I'm one of your Physics 100 students, and I'm writing to you in regard to a speech Dean Rubenstein made at orientation. He said, "Take the initiative to get to know your professors. They're real people too and they're interested in getting to know you, if you give them a chance." This seemed like a good idea. So I thought I'd drop you a line to let you know that my office hours are 8 to 12 on Friday nights, wherein I play anime DVDs on my 24-inch flat panel monitor. Feel free to bring chips and soda, and if comfort is a concern, a chair.

Rollo

Getting to know one or more of your professors is one of the best learning experiences you can have in college. There are a number of ways to do this. You could invite them to lunch, propose a project for them to supervise, or offer to do research.

The easiest way to make initial contact is to go to the professor's office hours. Some professors not-so-secretly hope that no one will show up. Others measure their popularity by whether students drop in, and are praying for someone to come by. Either way, from your point of view, it shouldn't matter. Office hours are for you, end of story.

Do some prep work to make the most of your time with the professor. Here are a few guidelines to keep in mind:

Try to master the material on your own first. Don't ask for help until you've done the reading or tried the problem sets. You want to discuss what the reading *means*, not what the reading *is*.

Come with specific questions. If you want feedback on a paper, bring the paper with you. Don't just ask, "What was wrong with this paper?" Be more specific: "How could I have made my introduction clearer?" or "Do you think that second example helps get my point across?"

Be clear about whether you are discussing a grade or asking for help. It's not wrong or unreasonable to ask a professor about a grade. But don't pretend to be asking for help when what you really want to do is argue a grade. If you do want to talk about a grade, there are better and worse ways to begin. Don't say, "This grade is wrong." Instead say, "I wanted to understand better the reasoning behind my grade. I was surprised by it, and wanted to get a better sense of the criteria. Is that something we can discuss?"

It's okay to say, "I still don't understand." Sure, you want your professor to think you're smart. But far more important is that you learn something and that you're able to succeed in the course. Be persistent if things still seem unclear to you: "I'm trying really hard, but I still don't get how to approach these word problems. Could you talk me through how you think about them?"

Using Your Academic Advisor

Academic advising varies, depending on the school and depending on the advisor. Your advisor may be a professor, administrator, or graduate student. They may or may not know much about the academic areas you're interested in. They may be a fantastic resource or of little help at all.

No matter how strong your advisor is, remember that you alone are responsible for your academic choices and for knowing the requirements. Advisors may know the system, but they usually have to look after a number of students. The only student you have to look after is yourself. So double-check to make sure that your advisor gets things right.

You should be a full participant in your advising sessions. As with professors, don't be afraid to ask lots of questions. Ask specific questions, like how a particular course will affect your workload or whether there are alternative ways to meet a requirement. But ask general questions too: "What was it like when you were a student?" "What are your thoughts on learning?" "What's your philosophy on how to get the most out of school?"

Talk to your advisor not only about your hopes, but also about your fears. Your advisor may be a good person to be open with about how you really feel about school: "I sometimes feel overwhelmed." "I'm still having trouble figuring out what I want to do with my life." "I'm doing well academically, but I'm not making any friends." Advisors are people too (just like professors); if you let them see what's really going on in your life, they may be able to help, and you might make a real connection in the process.

Of course, much of your conversation with your advisor will center on figuring out what courses to take. Come to your course selection meeting well prepared. That means having eight or ten courses picked out to discuss—not two, and not twenty-two. As we've said earlier, listen especially carefully about matters of placement, and seek out further information from a specific academic department if you're not satisfied with your placement advice.

THE MINOR MATTER OF MAJORS

There are two sorts of college educations: those that prepare you for a very specific postcollege endeavor and those that prepare you for anything (or, depending on your point of view, nothing). Although they may not know it, the majority of college students fall into the latter category.

You might be surprised to learn that you don't need a degree in poli sci or to be pre-law to go to law school. You don't need to major in economics to go into business or sales, or even to go to business school. You don't need to major in communication to work in TV or journalism or advertising or film. And you don't need to major in English to become an English teacher. For any of the above, and in fact for the great majority of jobs and graduate schools, you can major in almost anything.

Of course, to go to med school, you have to fulfill pre-med requirements (though you don't need to major in a science). And to get a graduate degree in, say, economics or physics or linguistics, you will be expected to have taken a number of courses in that area as an undergraduate, and you may or may not be expected to major in it, depending on the field and depending on the school.

You should also know that even if you have a complete change of heart after graduation, and decide you want to be a doctor even though you didn't go near a science course as an undergraduate, there's still hope. A growing number of students take a fifth year, sometimes after working in the real world for a while, during which they knock out their pre-med classes. Or they take a night school class in accounting or a class in computer programming before applying to business school, and so forth. The point is that while what you major in is important, in most cases, it doesn't keep you from doing what you want when you graduate.

My Four Majors

Some students show up to college and promptly announce to the world that they are going to quadruple-major: engineering, because of my love of "building things"; English, so I can be a writer if I want; political science in case I want to become a senator; and classics, because every well-rounded person should know how to speak Latin.

This is a bad idea. There's nothing wrong with having lots of interests. In fact, that's a blessing. It's possible that your school may let you double-major, or have a major and a minor. In general, though, you should use the experience of choosing a major as an exercise in making choices. A good reason for a double major is if you absolutely love two different fields of study and are willing and excited to take on whatever extra work that entails. A bad reason is that you just can't decide between two equally appealing majors.

But I Don't Like Anything

The flip side of liking too many academic areas is liking none at all. This is a surprisingly common problem, and one that is too rarely mentioned in official college material on choosing a major.

There's no doubt that college is a more enjoyable experience if you're excited about your major, and you're more likely to do well if you enjoy what you're studying and find it rewarding. Majors comprise anywhere from a quarter to a half of all your courses, and that's a lot of time to spend on something you aren't interested in. But simply saying it's better if you like your major doesn't make it any more likely that you will. If you haven't found an area you really like, there are a few things that are useful to keep in mind.

First, it's helpful to know the reasoning behind the requirement to have a major. It's not to punish you, although it can sometimes feel that way. Nor is it based on an assumption that everybody must love something. In a sense, it's the opposite. Educators feel strongly that, whether or not a student has a deep interest in a subject area, everyone should have the experience of learning a field in depth.

There are benefits to learning a subject in depth beyond just learning "a lot of facts about it." By taking many courses in the same area, you learn the modes of thought behind the academic discipline; you learn where the field has contributed to human understanding and what the open questions are; you are exposed to different and contrasting perspectives on similar material.

So when you major in something, you're not only learning the subject matter, you're learning about what it means to learn an academic discipline—*any* academic discipline—in depth. That kind of learning will benefit you whether or not you're in love with the area of study. Pick your major thoughtfully, but don't get fooled into thinking there's a right or wrong choice.

"But My Parents Want Me to Major In . . ."

How should you handle it if your parents want you to major in something that's different from what you want to major in? It's a tough issue, and we discuss it at length in Chapter 8. That chapter is all about you and your parents, and how to deal with the inevitable conflicts that come up.

The grades you receive in your first semester represent only a slice of what your transcript will look like by the time you graduate. Just as building a social life takes time, so does building an academic life. It takes time to get to know professors and to learn the skills involved in writing college papers, labs, and exams. It takes practice to feel comfortable participating in class.

But it's worth it. Reaching your academic potential requires patience, persistence, and a few good study skills. And that's the subject of the next chapter.

4
Studying

From: Sweeney
To: Duncan
Sent: Sunday, October 24, 1:44 AM
Subject: stupid profs

I just found out my American history midterm is tomorrow!! Supposedly, we were told this months ago, like I'm supposed to remember that?!

I have exactly 9 hours to learn everything that happened between 1492 and 1850. That gives me 1.4 minutes for each year! If I want to take a dump I have to skip 1677 through 1684. Is this someone's idea of a good way to teach!? Does my professor not know that some of us have a little thing I like to call "a life"? If the first half of the course is so important, why cram it all into the first half of the course? Why not give us time to savor it?

Damn. I better get to work. Quick quiz for you: Who said, "Dude, where are we?" Columbus. See, even he didn't know anything about American history.

Severely concerned,
Sweeney

Sweeney's got a long night ahead of him. No doubt, you'll have nights like this too. In this chapter, we look at three key hurdles along the road to academic success: procrastination, perfectionism, and performance anxiety. We'll look at how we get ourselves into these messes, and the best ways out. At the end of the chapter, we'll give you some important study tips that don't require much extra time but can make a huge difference.

THE PERILS OF PROCRASTINATION

Nearly everyone struggles with procrastination. Can't get started, can't stick with it. Even worse, the procrastination leads to a vicious cycle: you wait until the last minute, go all out to meet the deadline, and then end up completely exhausted. No wonder you can't get started on the next project. The last one nearly killed you. And for all the trouble, the work you turned in was rushed and your grades suffered.

Not surprisingly, Sweeney did poorly on that history midterm, his professor encouraged him to enroll in a study habits workshop, where Sweeney was asked to chart his work habits for a week. Here's his journal:

SWEENEY'S STUDY JOURNAL: 11/08–11/12

MONDAY:
Started doing some American history reading. Got hyper, so went over to Oak's room. His whole room is wallpapered with aluminum foil.

TUESDAY:
Worked on chemistry problem set. Didn't feel inspired, so Oak and me went over to Cube's room and watched the Pistons destroy the Sixers. Cube looks like a cube.

WEDNESDAY:
Nothing due tomorrow. Couldn't get off the mark. Real question is, will it even help if I study? I may be too far gone in econ to catch up. Better just to cram at the end?

THURSDAY:
Faced tough choice: read the sociology chapter or spend the evening with Jen. I understand neither of them, but Jen's insanely attractive and sociology isn't. You make the call.

FRIDAY:
Dude!

Let's take a look at some of the problems Sweeney runs into. Some of them may sound familiar.

Restlessness: *"Got hyper"*

Some people have more nervous energy than others and find it particularly hard to settle down at the beginning of studying. Why? The J Curve. When you first sit down to try to get into the material, your happiness level plummets. This is the time when you understand the material the least, and the whole evening stretches infinitely and painfully in front of you. In the first fifteen minutes, the urge to get up and do almost anything else is intense.

But as you start to get into it, your happiness level slowly starts to climb. "Hmm. I'm kind of starting to understand this. This is actually sort of interesting." A sense of accomplishment kicks in, and before you know it, you're happier than you were before you started.

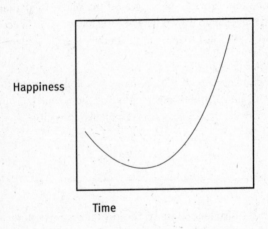

The key? Don't get up during the first half hour no matter how little you are understanding, no matter how hyper you feel, and no matter how much you're convinced that you really need to have a drink of water, go for a walk, or buy a new set of gel pens. You should *assume* you'll have thoughts like, "I don't understand this!" "Why are they making me do all this work?" and, "It'll be easier if I wait a month."

Instead of taking those as signs to stop studying, take them as signs to sit tight and slow down. Do whatever helps you gain some understanding, no matter how slowly it's going. Slog through the pages even if you're not getting it yet, read through your class notes, write down things you don't understand or questions to ask the professor or TA.

Assume that the first half hour is not for getting through the material quickly, but for getting over the hump of getting started. Once you start to gain a sense of what's going on, some of the nervous energy dissipates.

If the restlessness is overpowering, get some exercise before you head to the library. If you find the restlessness is still incapacitating despite your best efforts to deal with it, you might want to consult a doctor or therapist—it's possible that you have attention deficit disorder or some other learning concern.

The Zone: *"Didn't feel inspired"*

We all know those magical times, whether in academics, sports, or anything else, when you're in the "zone" and performing better than you ever thought possible. But those moments are rare, and as the J Curve suggests, super unlikely when you first sit down. You can't wait to feel inspired in order to write a paper or complete a problem set. It's like sports: if you happen to be inspired at the right moment, great. But game time is game time, and getting things done often means working when you're not inspired, working when you're not at your best, and working when the going gets tough. Being productive is not about how you feel, it's about what you do.

Adrenaline Junkie: *"Nothing due tomorrow"*

For the veteran procrastinator, getting started can be even harder because you're dependent on the adrenaline of a deadline to gather the energy and concentration to get things done.

Help comes in two forms. First, if you are dead set on using panic as your only form of motivation, then you'll just have to find ways to feel panic sooner. Think about it. When you wait until the very last minute to study, you aren't thinking, "Gosh, now I really need to buckle down"; you're thinking, "Holy crap!! I should have started this project two months ago!" Well, it's two months ago *right now*. Feel panicked.

The second thing you can do is find alternative motivations. The adrenal jolt of sheer panic isn't the only thing that gets people going. Sometimes it helps to use a form of self-competition. Give yourself targets and see if you can hit them. Even though it's not due for two weeks, challenge yourself to crank out a first draft of your paper by 10:00 p.m. tonight. Or pair up with a friend and agree that you're going to study twenty hours this week, no matter what.

Fun: *"Jen or sociology?"*

This is perhaps the toughest obstacle that Sweeney encounters. You see your choice as, "Would I rather hook up with the person of my dreams, or do my sociology assignment?" No one in human history has ever happily chosen the latter. Even lesser temptations have their pull, whether it's eating pizza, going to the gym, watching a video, talking with a friend, playing the guitar, or simply not studying.

Here's a thought experiment: given the choice between eating a marshmallow now and waiting for ten minutes to get two marshmallows, which would you do? Amazingly, if you were four years old, your answer to this question would strongly correlate to how you would do on your SATs twelve years later.* Exactly why is unclear, but those children who were able to wait for two marshmallows in ten minutes scored far higher on the exam.

It's probably related to self-discipline and your ability to delay gratification now for a bigger future reward. So what's the answer, Jen or sociology? Truth is, you have to make time for both. If you choose Jen every time, you're going to flunk out. On the other hand, if your life is all about delayed gratification and you never do things you like, you'll burn out.

There's enough time in the day to do some of the things you like and still do a good amount of studying. If you find that your schedule is heavily tipped to all fun or all work, eventually it will catch up with you. Over the long haul, you should strive for balance.

Overwhelmed: *"I don't understand the material . . . too far gone"*

Throughout this book, we try to avoid simplistic advice. But on the matter of falling behind, there's really only one way to put it: don't. *DO NOT.*

Remember, if it's overwhelming now, it's going to be even more overwhelming when you're working on it at the last minute, under the burden of learning weeks of material all at once. The place to get hold of a course is at the very beginning. If, despite your best efforts, you're having trouble either keeping up or understanding the material, talk to your advisor

*Daniel Goleman, *Emotional Intelligence* (New York: Bantam Books, 1995).

or the professor and get it straightened out *within the first three weeks of the semester.*

If you aren't sure whether you should be asking for help, then go to your professor or TA and discuss it. You can say, "I feel like I'm not totally understanding the material. Can you help me figure out whether I'm doing something wrong, or if I'm overplaced, or whether I should get additional help?"

If you are already behind ("It's the middle of the semester. Why didn't they tell me this earlier?"), spend a couple of hours on your own or with an advisor and make a plan. Divide the job of catching up into smaller tasks that you can accomplish one sitting at a time. You didn't fall behind all at once, and you can't catch up all at once.

In the end, the old cliché is true: slow and steady wins the race. Not "slow, drunk, and steady" or "annoyed, sleepy, and hyper." Just slow and steady.

Time Management

A few final thoughts on Sweeney's study habits:

Uni-tasking. Sweeney is fooling himself if he thinks he's going to be able to study and do anything else simultaneously (with the possible exception of listening to music). Yes, you can keep up with instant messaging while surfing the Net and watching TV, but studying takes your entire brain.

It's tempting to try to figure out ways to make studying more pleasant, whether that means having the television on or studying in a coffee shop. But the single best way to make studying more pleasant is to get over the J Curve and into the work, and you do that by eliminating distractions, not adding them. If you try to multitask, you're likely to spend three or four hours doing work that should have taken an hour. Better to work and then hang out, or hang out and then work.

Big blocks versus small chunks. Is it better to study in big blocks of time or small chunks? The answer is big blocks. If you try to write a paper or complete a problem set during a half hour here and twenty minutes there, your work will suffer. You need time to immerse yourself in the material and cover some ground, even if you're taking breaks every once in a while.

At the same time, it's a mistake to think you can't get anything accomplished in the half hour between classes or before dinner. If you have a half hour, find tasks that take twenty minutes: Review your notes from class. Do a bit of recommended reading. While carving out big blocks each night is the key to success, the small chunks add up. If you use them wisely, you'll have more time during the week to do the things you enjoy.

THE IMPERFECTION OF PERFECTIONISM

Perfectionism isn't about doing things well; it's not about proofreading your paper before you turn it in or trying your hardest on your problem set. It's a way of coping with anxiety. In high school, it can work. In college, it doesn't.

There's stress involved in taking on any new task. Like Sweeney, some people deal with that stress by simply putting the task off for as long as possible. Other people go in the other direction, beating anxiety by gaining complete control and mastery over the task. Every last detail is put in place, every nook and cranny explored. There's nothing inherently wrong with that. But in practice, it can lead to several problems.

All or Nothing

The all-or-nothing syndrome is at play when you work hard on something for as long as you can stay completely on top of it, but if you slide even a little, you give up. Or you decide in advance that since you can't go at it 100 percent, you won't try at all.

You don't have enough time to give your room an industrial-strength cleaning—eliminating every last dirt molecule and killing every last dust mite—so why bother picking up the clothes off the floor? It's odd to think that an excessively sloppy room is the result of perfectionism, but often it is.

The academic version of the sloppy room is deciding that if you can't read every single page of assigned work in your Russian novels course, you won't read any. If you can't get your chemistry homework to print out so that all the margins are perfectly aligned, you won't bother with how it looks at all. Too often, the goal of perfection blocks us from doing *anything*.

The Eighty-Twenty Trap

Another problem is that in striving for perfection, you end up spending 80 percent of your allotted time making the first 20 percent of the task absolutely perfect, and are forced to rush through the last 80 percent of the task in 20 percent of the time. Your paper ends up with an awesome introduction, and not much else. Or you master tomorrow's irregular verbs for Spanish class, at the expense of doing any of your geology assignment. The compulsion to be perfect keeps you from making smart decisions about how to spend your time.

Instant Messenger

Craigster: I am sooo learning this chemistry material!

Lil5Mackie: How far are you?

Craigster: I'm about a third of the way finished.

Lil5Mackie: You've been studying this for five days! Don't you have other finals?

Craigster: But I'm really learning it.

Lil5Mackie: You're gonna get an A+++ on the first third of your chem exam, and fail everything else!

Craigster: Hmm . . . you have a point. Okay, gotta run. Must study.

Burnout

Finally, while perfectionism is an attempt to reduce stress by staying in control, it inevitably creates its own stresses. It's sort of like trying to find Catherine Zeta-Jones in the phone book by starting with the A's and reading every name. It's an okay way to find a friend in the high school yearbook, but not so great for finding someone in greater Los Angeles. You'll feel good that you're going step-by-step, leaving no stone unturned, but you'll give up long before the task is complete.

CONQUERING PERFECTIONISM

What helps when perfectionism is getting in the way? Here are a few suggestions:

Do a brain dump. In *Bird by Bird*,* a book of advice for writers, novelist Anne Lamott extols the virtues of what she

*Anne Lamott, *Bird by Bird* (New York: Anchor Books, 1995).

calls "shitty first drafts." Blast through a first draft, getting your ideas down in whatever form they come out. Don't worry about grammar, organization, style, or spelling. Your goal is to outwit that perfectionist editor in your head, the one that tells you to rewrite that first sentence a thousand different ways. Once you've dumped whatever is in your head onto the page, then you've at least got a first draft, and shitty though it may be, it's always easier to edit a draft than to work from nothing.

Polish last. If you're at work on a paper or other creative project, think of yourself as a sculptor with a piece of marble. Chisel the big chunks to make the statue's head, torso, and limbs before you focus on getting the nose or fingernails just right. Once you've got the general form of the assignment figured out, then you can focus on the nitty-gritty. Don't leave the details out, but don't spend time polishing before you even know what's in or out, or what the big picture looks like.

Embrace the struggle. Being good at college means being okay with the feeling of not quite understanding something. It's fine to be obsessed with mastering a concept, but don't let that obsession get in the way of moving on to the next concept, and the next. Some things are learnable on the first pass through, and some aren't. Sometimes, what you're learning is the process of learning itself—how to ask the right questions and how to live with uncertainty. There will be times when it's best to think to yourself, "I sort of understand this, I've put in a reasonable amount of time on it and done my best, and now it's time to work on something else."

PERFORMANCE ANXIETY: THE FEAR OF FEAR ITSELF

From: Rollo
To: Mom
Sent: Monday, December 13, 9:35 PM
Subject: finals

Dearest Mother,

Could you please send me a few "good vibes" for my econ final at exactly 10:00 AM, eastern standard time? There is always a small but worrisome chance I will "lose it" like at my fifth grade trumpet recital.

Your son,
Rollo

Do you have anxiety when you take tests? You look around the exam room and see that it is full of students who are not only smarter than you, but better rested and better prepared. How did you get into this mess?

We can't attest to your level of preparation, but we can tell you that you aren't in a room full of brilliant super-students who are immune to stress. If you feel nervous and under-rested, so do many others. If misery loves company, then there's a lot of love in those exam rooms.

The Paradox of Falling Asleep

Sleep helps. You should try to get plenty of it throughout the semester, but especially the couple of nights before an exam. The problem is this: the more you *try* to fall asleep, the more stressed you get if you can't.

What to do? You have to make sure (sorry, here it is again) to study for the exam *before* the night before. If you're already prone to having trouble sleeping, last-minute studying will just make you anxious about all the things you don't know. Having some closure on your studying before the hours leading up to the exam can help you relax and fall asleep more easily.

Whatever you do, don't use the time between turning off the lights and actually falling asleep to review facts and equations in your mind. Once lights are out, make thinking about the material off-limits. It won't help you remember anything, and it will keep you awake. (By the way, if you can't fall asleep because you're worried about oversleeping, buy a second alarm clock for five dollars and put it across the room.)

During the Test

It is true that tests tend to count more in college than in high school because there are fewer of them. But don't be fooled into thinking each test is some sort of make-or-break situation. Any given test, even a final, is likely to be worth less than half of your overall grade, and each grade is only one grade out of thirty-two or more courses you'll take in college. No individual test turns out to be all that important.

In addition, college exams tend to be longer than high school exams, so there's more time to recover from initial panic. They also tend to emphasize understanding instead of memory. Sure, there are facts to learn, but exams also require reasoning and analysis—and those things are less affected by anxiety. Your professor will likely forgive the fact that you blanked on Napoleon's name so long as your analysis of his rise to power is thoughtful and clear.

Answer the actual question asked. When taking an exam, some students make the mistake of failing to address the specifics of the test question. If the question requires you to compare and contrast the leadership styles of Winston Churchill and FDR, don't simply ruminate about the two leaders in general, or about leadership in general. Go directly to the heart of the question: "This essay will discuss two ways in which Churchill's and FDR's leadership styles were similar, and three ways in which they were different." Most professors favor a clear, direct style over one that is rambling or florid.

Keep going. Most students find that their anxiety dissipates once they look through the exam and start working on it. But what if you draw a blank on the very first question on the test? Two words: move on. Jot down what you do remember, leave some space for coming back to it, and move on to the next question. Don't waste time wondering whether that first question is important. Get going on the next question, or the next, and come back later if you have time. Once you get into a groove on a question that feels easier, you're off and running.

Write *something*. If you're running out of time and still haven't gotten to the last question, it is worth taking the last couple of minutes to outline an answer, even if you don't write it out in full. Write down whatever you think will help the professor recognize that you actually know the material. Don't worry about presentation and writing style; get right to the most interesting couple of thoughts you have on the subject.

SMALL INVESTMENT, BIG PAYOFF: SIX TIPS FOR STUDYING SMART

Once you're in the chair studying, there are specific things you can do that don't take much if any extra time or effort, but that can have big payoffs in terms of learning and excelling.

1. Study in Groups

From: Macani
To: PJ
Sent: Wednesday, January 5, 5:45 PM
Subject: Gracias

Hey Peej,

This is an official thank you for "Take Macani to the Library" month. I got a B+ on my Spanish 1 final! I don't think you understand the significance of this grade. This is the class where everyone else already knows Spanish and lived in Venezuela or Peru or wherever for ten years, and the teacher is talking to us in Spanish the whole time, saying the Spanish version of "blahblahblah," as if I *know* Spanish, and I always want to say, "I'm sorry, I don't know Spanish, that's why I'm taking this class."

Buenos noches, mi pollo,
Macani

Macani and PJ, without knowing it, have actually hit on a great way to study. Studying is like working out: if a friend is involved, you're more likely to go. And once you've finished a problem set or reading assignment, one of the best ways to really engage with the material is to discuss it with friends and classmates. Talking about the material makes it more interesting and helps you remember it; and since different people have different strengths, you can answer each other's questions.

Of course, it's important to do individual assignments individually. Clarify with your professor or TA in each class what kind of collaboration is permitted. Some classes might permit you to collaborate on, say, a problem set with some classmates as long as you do your own written work. Others ask that you do work solely on your own and only look to your TA for assistance.

2. "Study" the Syllabus

One of the best study resources for understanding the big picture is the syllabus. Don't think of it as merely a bunch of reading assignments; think of it as the blueprint for the course. It gives you a sense for how the professor is organizing the course as a whole, and how various topics fit together. When studying for exams, start by studying the syllabus. Imagine that your midterm or final will include the following question: "Why is the syllabus organized the way it is and what does that tell us about my view of what we are learning?" Often, this question will yield rich insights.

3. Ask Yourself: "Why Are We Reading This?"

Let's imagine that your professor assigns Sigmund Freud's *The Interpretation of Dreams*. The way you read it will depend in part on the subject matter of the course. It will be read for different purposes depending on whether you're taking a course in psychology, philosophy, feminism, the cultural history of Vienna, or expository writing.

At the same time, even within a particular field, there are any number of reasons a text might be assigned. The mistake is to think you're being asked to read *The Interpretation of Dreams* because you're supposed to "learn" it. You *are* supposed to learn it, but you need a more specific purpose in mind. Are you reading it so that you can master how dreams are interpreted (unlikely)? To see how Freud constructs an argument? To learn certain particularly important concepts from Freud's thinking? Are you reading it in comparison to how other psychologists interpret this subject, or neuroscientists, or novelists, or painters? Is it being compared to other works by Freud? To your own experience of dreams? Are you being asked to consider the book's contribution to intellectual history, or is the purpose to uncover underlying assumptions—and flaws—in Freud's thinking?

Your answers to these questions will help you target your reading. Rather than reading and looking for everything, you're reading to answer specific questions. That usually means reading certain parts of the book in more depth than others. In the end, that not only saves you time, but helps you pay attention to what is most important.

4. Find the Right Role for Your Own Opinions

What role do your own thoughts, views, and life experiences play when studying social sciences and humanities? In answering this question, there are two key mistakes to avoid. The first is assuming that your view doesn't matter at all. The second is allowing your own view to cloud your understanding of what the author is really trying to say.

It's easy to push your opinions out of the equation when you're reading an assignment. Anyone who writes something that gets published and assigned, you reason, must be brilliant and untouchable.

It's true that, by and large, you're reading the works of profound thinkers and great writers. But all thinking and writing happens in a context. If what you're reading makes assertions or observations that don't accord with your own experience of the world—or that do—that's significant. These are trails worth following.

On the other hand, the right to critique a work has to be "earned." You earn that right by understanding the work on its own terms, and by understanding the contribution that it made or continues to make. If you don't understand why Shakespeare's insights into what motivates the human soul are considered significant, you're going to have trouble persuading anyone that your own insights on the subject are worth listening to. Look first for the brilliance in what you're studying, for what seems thought-provoking, profound, or true. If you've worked hard to do that, then the ways that you see things differently take on real meaning.

5. Don't Gloss Over Contradictions

One of the biggest mistakes first-year college students make is to assume that things are supposed to fit neatly together, or that if you develop an argument, it has to account for everything. In fact, one of the surest signs of academic maturity is to be honest about your argument's limits—the exceptions, the open questions, the ways in which your theory doesn't quite work.

If, for example, you are arguing in a history of science class that science progresses primarily as the result of individual genius, you should also consider what you see as exceptions to this. What is the role of institutional support or historical forces? Often students think that considering such questions will weaken or destroy their thesis. But your goal is not to put forward only that which supports your thesis. Your goal is to say what is true, and usually truth contains complexity and contradiction.

6. In Math and Science, Do Practice Problems

Math and science courses in college can be very different from how they were in high school. In high school you can get by with what some students refer to as "plug and chug." In other words, if you memorize the formula, principle, or theory and input the information correctly (being careful with notation), you will get the right answer to the problem.

In college, you are more likely to be called on to understand what the formula, principle, or theory actually represents. Remembering a formula is important, but it's not enough. You might be asked to apply a formula in a novel situation, or to combine different principles to solve a problem, or to recognize a situation in which a theory does not apply. In addition to memorizing, you'll be asked questions to demonstrate understanding.

Thus, one of the keys to doing well in math and science is to work through lots of practice problems. Do the ones assigned, but periodically, and especially when studying for an exam, do problems that have not been assigned. The more problems you do, the more you'll see patterns in approaches, and the more comfortable you'll feel.

A NOTE ON PLAGIARISM

Plagiarism—using other people's ideas or words and claiming them as your own by failing to cite their work—is one of the most strictly punished offenses in college. It can mean failing a course or getting thrown out of school.

Why do people plagiarize? Here are the three most common reasons.

1. "I didn't know it was plagiarism." Rules about plagiarism may vary slightly from college to college, and rules about collaboration can vary from class to class. What doesn't vary is that it is your responsibility to learn what the rules are and to follow them. Not knowing the rules is not an excuse.

2. "I panicked. I was stuck." Many students who plagiarize do so because they feel stuck. The paper is due in three hours, and it's only half finished. Cheating feels like the only way out. It's not.

Obviously, the best way to avoid this problem is to plan ahead. If you feel overwhelmed by your schoolwork, talk as early as possible to a professor, TA, or counselor. Colleges deal with these issues all the time.

But what if it's too late for that? You're gripped by panic, can't think straight, and realize there's no way to get the paper in on time. No matter what it feels like to you in the moment, don't plagiarize. It's always better to deal with the consequences, if any, of turning something in late than to risk the potentially much larger penalties for cheating.

3. "I won't get caught." If you're one of those people who in high school grabbed things off the Internet and turned them in as your own, college is the time to stop. If you think taking something off the Internet is not considered plagiarism, you're wrong. It is plagiarism, every bit as much as copying something out of a book. If you know it's cheating but assume you won't get caught, you should reconsider that assumption. If you can find something on the Internet or in a book, your professor can too. Reconsider the ethics involved as well. Is getting by worth the stress and burden of knowing you cheated?

The bottom line on studying is to get out of the gate early. The pain and discipline involved in staying on top of assignments are far easier to handle than the panic and frustration of trying to play catch-up. If you study some each day, it will make a big difference in your academic performance. And just as important, you'll know you did your best.

5
Identity

From: PJ
To: nobody
Sent: Sunday, December 5, 1:12 AM
Subject: thinking

Dear nobody:

Someday I'll have the guts to send this e-mail to someone. I don't know who. But someone.

I'm not really sure how I know this or how long I've known this but . . . I think I'm gay. It even feels strange to write that. I'm gay.

I don't even know how to explain that I know. It's like shaking an Etch A Sketch backwards, where shaking it makes the picture clearer. And as I look back on my life, everything starts to make sense. Girls I had a crush on in middle school, why I hated the senior prom, why I hate it when my mother goes on and on about whether I'm dating anyone.

Hmm. I wonder if other people know. Maybe that's why my

field hockey coach in high school kept asking me if I "wanted to talk to her about something." God, I hated that. Maybe other people have always thought so and never said anything? Well, PJ, what do I do now? I guess I don't need to do anything. This is stupid, writing to myself.

PJ (me)

THE DECK RESHUFFLED: THE CHALLENGE OF IDENTITY

Identity challenges aren't on anyone's daily schedule: "wake up; eat breakfast; attend class; figure out who I am; take nap." There's no identity exam to pass, no graduation requirement to meet.

Still, the challenges are real. You sit in your political theory class wondering whether, as the only Latino student in your section, people expect you to share your views on affirmative action. You talk with a friend about what really matters in life, and find yourself suddenly uncertain. You lie awake at night trying to find some way to accept aspects of yourself that make you uncomfortable. Like so much of the rest of college, the struggles can be profound, overwhelming, and confusing.

In a sense this whole book is about identity. You have a social identity, an academic identity, a sexual identity. You're a certain way with your roommate, a certain way with your parents. But identity can be about other things as well. It can be about growing up in a small town or a big city. It can be about your parents' divorce, your grandfather's journey to America, or feeling like a social outcast in junior high. It can be about race, ethnicity, sexual orientation, social class, religious beliefs, abilities and disabilities, or cultural values. It can be about pride or shame, isolation or belonging.

The best way to get into the tough questions of identity is by looking at some examples. We'll take a look at two of the most complex issues—race and (coming back to PJ) sexual orientation.

RACE AND ETHNICITY

From an identity standpoint, what does it mean to "be" something? To be white, to be Pakistani, to be Catholic? What determines membership in a group, or exclusion from it? What is the relationship between your individual identity and group identity? How do other people's expectations of you factor into how you see yourself? How is being a member of a minority group different from being a member of a majority group?

Macani struggles with some of these questions:

From: Macani
To: Craig
Sent: Thursday, November 18, 10:11 PM
Subject: What's HAPA-ning?

Hey Craig,

So, I went to the first meeting of the Half Asian Persons Association today. The group's sort of serious and sort of not serious, which is maybe about right.

I don't know. Sometimes I wonder if I'm supposed to feel confused about who I really am and where I belong. Or maybe I'm supposed to feel lucky because I get to be "ethnically ambiguous." But I don't really feel either of those. I feel outside of the whole thing, even outside of the biracial thing. I mean, everyone thinks my name is Japanese, and they're surprised when I tell them I'm named after my mother's college roommate, who was from Nigeria. So what does that tell you? I don't know.

Oh, and get this. Rollo asked me if he could join HAPA. I was like, "You're not half Asian," and he was like, "Well, I'm only one half less half Asian than you." I guess he's right. It's always about meeting girls, isn't it?

Macani

How do you sort through the confusion and anxiety and stay on a constructive path? Here are some thoughts that might help.

Accept Complexity

Feeling comfortable with your identity doesn't require you to make a choice among different aspects of yourself. If you feel pulled in different directions, the tension itself may be a part of who you are. The real you is the one with the questions, the one whose identity feels settled one day and unsettled the next.

After all, a lot of things go into you being you, and those factors often cut across labels and affiliations. A white student and a Chinese American student might each have grown up in a family with a severely disabled sibling. That, as much as anything else, has shaped how they see the world and how they see themselves. Despite all the ways they are different from each other, it would not be surprising if they found they had a lot in common.

The flip side of this is true as well: *within* groups there can be enormous diversity. How is the identity of a Latino student whose father works as a janitor at a high school in Los Angeles different from the identity of a Latino student whose mother is the principal of that same school? How are both of their identities different from that of a Latino student who grew up in New York City, or San Antonio, or the Dominican Republic? There will be similarities, to be sure, but important differences as well.

The long and short of it is this: some aspects of who you are will complement each other, while others won't quite make sense together. As you move along on the path of self-discovery, some of that will change and some of it won't. Complexity is an inherent part of this terrain. That's not a matter of being in college; that's a matter of being human.

Balance Internal and External Expectations

Your identity isn't something that gets imposed on you from your family or from a campus group or from the media. You shouldn't conform to what others expect you to be solely to please them. But external expectations have an important role to play. If your parents want you to go to church while you're at college, you can make your own choice about whether to oblige. Just don't dismiss their request out of hand: "They don't know me. That's not who I am." Instead, use their expectations as a chance to learn. What has going to church meant to them in their lives? What does it mean *for them* if you do or don't go to church? What do your parents know that you don't? How has the world changed since they were your age? How has it stayed the same?

It's a matter of balance. If you are too influenced by outside expectations, you might lose—or never develop—your own internal compass. Other people may know more about the world than you do, but you know more about yourself. As you sort through what others want and expect of you, be keenly aware of your own intuitions and values, and work hard to find what you want for yourself. It's important to listen to the voices of others, but ultimately, your goal is to find your own.

Explore Personal Experiences

College students often assume that conversations about issues like race and identity should center on things bigger than themselves, like history and culture, sociology and economics. Sometimes they should, but personal experiences matter too. They don't define or limit you, but they contribute to who you are and how you see things. Whether you're trying to get a better sense for where you fit in or trying to explain your views to a friend, life experiences—stories from your past—can be a good place to start.

Sweeney and Duncan had an interesting instant messenger exchange involving race. They take on some hard issues, but soon get stuck.

Instant Messenger

Sweeneee: Whaaaat? Why did you join a black frat?
Dunk431: Well, you joined a "white" frat.

Sweeneee: I didn't join a white frat. I joined a regular frat.

Dunk431: It's a white frat.

Sweeneee: It's an anything frat. There's a black guy, an Asian guy, and a guy that I don't know what he is. It doesn't matter what race people are. If you're cool you can be in it.

Dunk431: If race doesn't matter, why didn't you join a black frat?

Sweeneee: If they wanted me, I would.

Dunk431: Oh, come on. You know you wouldn't feel comfortable in a frat where you were the only white guy.

Sweeneee: Dunk, I want to be in a frat that anyone can join. And I am. And you're not.

Dunk431: Dude, in Hillside, everyone we knew was white except me, and so obviously, all our friends were white. But it's good to be around some other black guys for a change, you know? People who have some of the same experiences as me.

Sweeneee: The same experiences? Dude!! Who could have more similar experiences than me and you? We've known each other since forever. Think of all the white people I have nothing in common with (e.g., my roommate), and think of how similar you and me are.

Dunk431: I'm just saying it's good to be able to spend time with other black people. That doesn't seem like it should be so hard to understand. You spend time with other white people.

Sweeneee: Dude, they're not white people.

Dunk431: They're not white people?

Sweeneee: Well, not on purpose. It could be anyone.

Dunk431: It's different if you're black. Maybe that's what you don't understand.

Sweeneee: Yeah, you've had it tough in your big-ass house in the suburbs.

Dunk431: What is that supposed to mean!!??

Sweeneee: I don't know. What does any of this mean? I'm
saying I know you better than anyone, and you're black.
What's the difference?

Dunk431: Okay, man, this is getting stupid. Talk to that black
guy in your frat. He'll explain it.

In part, this conversation is about friendship, but it can
also be seen through the lens of identity and groups. Sweeney
believes that race need not be central to who you are or how
you see yourself. What really counts, he seems to be saying, is
who you are as an individual, the "content of your character."

Duncan sees it differently. He feels that race plays a substantial role in who he is. Though there may be differences
among individual black students, or Korean American students, or Latino students, there are also important similarities.
It's not one's race, per se, that matters, but the ways that society treats race. Group identity based on race is not about how
you look; it's about belonging to a group of people who have
certain shared experiences and a common heritage.

If Sweeney and Duncan come back to this conversation,
talking about important past experiences would be a good place
to start. They might, for example, talk about what happened at
camp many years ago. They attended the same day camp as
kids, and on the first day an ugly incident occurred down by the
pool. Sweeney's recollection is that two of the other kids
taunted Duncan about being black. Sweeney stuck up for his
friend, and the taunting stopped. Sweeney files the memory
away as "the time I stood up for Duncan." In any event, he
doesn't think about it much either way.

Duncan also remembers that Sweeney came to his aid,
but what stands out for him is the memory of intense feelings of

shame and anger. No one had treated him that way before; the sudden awareness of being different washed over him like a tidal wave. It was not merely an "event"; it was the first of several experiences in his life that shifted his core assumptions about people he didn't know. Instead of assuming people were good-hearted until proven otherwise, he assumed the opposite.

Through the years there were other incidents that stung—some clear-cut, some not. In some ways, the burden of wondering whether something was the result of prejudice or the result of other factors was as hard for Duncan as the incidents themselves. Did his high school football coach change him from quarterback to wide receiver because the other players at quarterback were better? Or was he shifted because he was black? Duncan was never sure.

Will discussing formative experiences like these settle the fraternity question that Sweeney and Duncan were arguing about? Probably not. But over time, the stark certainty that characterizes the first conversation may give way to an awareness that these questions are more complex than either person initially thought. Each will come to understand his own views better, and will develop greater empathy for the choices of the other.

SEXUAL ORIENTATION

Sexual orientation is another important identity issue. Many college students (and high school students and adults) experience some confusion about their sexuality, and as is so often the case with sex, these concerns are more common than people assume.

Self-Discovery

Most people struggle at one time or another with issues of self-acceptance. It could be related to looks, personality, or background. It could be about successes and failures, or regret over actions taken or not taken. Sexual orientation is a common arena for these struggles, partly because sexuality is an important aspect of who we are, and partly because of the complex and sometimes contradictory messages we get from the media, friends, and family.

Pulling apart the strands of your sexual self is complicated and can take time. In fact, it's a road you may be on the rest of your life. A key question is this: Can you love yourself along the way, when you feel weak as well as strong, ashamed as well as proud, confused as well as certain? It's a tough question, but it's crucial that you come to a place where the answer is yes.

You might wonder how you can love yourself even as you're engaged in the struggle to fully accept yourself. The answer isn't about pretending you feel something you don't; it's about understanding the meaning of unconditional love, and learning to nurture it in your relationship with yourself.

Unconditional love is the kind of love a parent feels for a child (and some people feel for their pets). Parents love their child even when the child feels sad, or ashamed, or unworthy of being loved. In fact, parents might feel an extra measure of compassion for a child during times like these, when the child needs a parent the most. Coming to terms with your sexual identity can be thrilling and fascinating, but it can also be lonely and rough. Wherever you are in the process, you will surely need support—from the people around you and also from yourself.

Coming Out, Staying In

For students who are gay, lesbian, bisexual, or transgendered, self-discovery soon leads to another set of questions: Should I tell anyone? If so, who and how?

There is little one-size-fits-all advice. Coming out is a personal choice, and everyone's situation is different. Often, those who come out to their friends and family report that it was a tremendous burden lifted and that being open about who they are has made their life more satisfying. But there are also stories of families thrown into crisis and friendships lost, which is why coming out can feel so threatening and often takes real courage.

Maybe the best advice is this: *before* you come out to someone important in your life, build a support network. Talk with a trusted friend, mentor, or campus group that understands these issues and can act as both support and sounding board. There's no substitute for having people on your side who really get what you're going through and who will support you no matter how things turn out.

Despite her own doubts that she ever would, PJ talked with Macani about the subject. The two had a brief conversation and, soon after, Macani wrote this e-mail to PJ:

From: Macani
To: PJ
Sent: Thursday, December 16, 10:31 PM
Subject: my reaction

Hey PJ:
I went looking for you after our talk, but I couldn't find you so I wanted to at least start the conversation by e-mail. I'm really,

really sorry if I upset you. I sooo didn't mean to. Just like you haven't come out to people very often, well, no one has ever come out to me, so it was a new experience for me too. I felt a little scared, and the stupid joke I made (about this being unlikely to solve all your relationship problems) was because I was nervous, and now that I think about it, I realize that was so not what you needed someone to say.

Anyway, if you didn't know it already, you're my best friend at school, and I hope you always will be, and I would do anything for you. The Two Musketeers forever.

Macani

Although it could have been worse, it would be reasonable for PJ to feel hurt by Macani's initial reaction. But remember, while the news is something PJ has thought about for a long time, it hits Macani all at once. A bunch of different thoughts rush through Macani's mind: "This makes me nervous." "What am I supposed to say?" "Why is she telling *me* this?" "Is she attracted to *me*?" In a panic, Macani resorts to her default mode and makes a joke.

Not One Conversation but Many

As Macani's e-mail demonstrates, coming out to someone is not one conversation but many conversations over time. Someone who has a nervous or negative initial reaction might shift their view and become more open as the news sinks in. And someone who is accepting at the outset might still have questions or concerns down the road.

In short order, PJ and Macani ended up becoming closer as a result of these conversations. In fact, Macani became part of PJ's support system as she prepared to tell her mother. Macani and PJ worked through the hard questions, like "What will happen if she gets really upset?" "What if she tells me how disappointed she is, or cuts me off?" They talked at length about what each response might mean for PJ and how she might find support.

At Christmas break, PJ decided to tell her mother. The reaction? "I suspected," her mother said. Her mother's demeanor became stern, and she started giving PJ "advice," but advice that felt to PJ more like an attack: "This is not a small thing, you know. This is not an easy life you're choosing."

"I'm not *choosing* it, Mom! This is who I am," PJ responded.

"Well, it affects a lot of other people too!" said her mother. "I'm telling you, this is not a small thing."

For a while they left it at that. But subsequent conversations improved, and PJ's mother shared some of the feelings that motivated her concerns. She told PJ that the hardest part for her was thinking that PJ had been struggling with this on her own, without motherly support. The good news is that over time, PJ and her mother developed a relationship that, while occasionally strained, felt to both of them more authentic and in many ways more mutually nourishing than their relationship had been previously.

People on the receiving end of surprising or difficult news often go through stages of reaction. Even the most loving parent might experience denial and anger before some form of acceptance sets in. You're giving your parents news about you, but it's about them too. It's also about your relationship, and about memories of the past and visions of the future. There's a lot to think about, a lot of reordering that needs to happen—and that takes time.

TALKING ACROSS DIFFERENCES

Whether the conversation is about race, gender, sexual orientation, religion, or politics, talking across differences is rarely easy. But it's crucial, to your college education as well as to the life of the community you live in. Too often the fear that these conversations will go poorly keeps us from having them all. That's why Sweeney and Duncan deserve a lot of credit for having their conversation about race. They haven't resolved anything, but they had the courage to dive into some tough issues.

Why are people afraid? Some students (typically "majority" students) worry that if they say the wrong thing they'll be labeled as prejudiced or narrow-minded, or be shunted aside as someone who just "doesn't get it." They may also worry that their point of view is not legitimate when it comes to talking about a group to which they don't belong, or that their life experiences don't count.

Other students (typically "minority" students) worry about being labeled as oversensitive, or as someone who sees everything through the lens of race or religion, gender or sexual orientation. The burden to have to educate the majority about minority views and concerns is a heavy one, and it's not hard to see why some students resent that role.

Regardless of where you stand, pretty much everyone worries that talking about divisive issues might hurt an otherwise good friendship. There's no secret formula for making these conversations easy or risk-free. But there are a few guidelines that can make them more likely to be productive.

1. Avoid Debating

Before you start a conversation, ask yourself what your goal is. Typically, we want to prove that our view is right; we want to change the other person's mind; we want to debate, and win. For many conversations, that makes sense; it's fun to argue, and college is a great place to sharpen your debating skills.

But in the context of tough issues, thinking of the conversation as a debate can lead to trouble. The tacit ground rules of debate are these: "I'll make my best arguments. Instead of listening to me, you should be planning your best arguments in response. Then when you're talking, I'll be planning my counterresponse." Little learning takes place in any direction, and frustration and misunderstanding often result.

2. Ask, "Why Do We See This Differently?"

Avoiding debate doesn't mean avoiding tough issues. Throw yourself into them, but shift your purpose from "winning" to "learning." Set aside your desire (for now) to have the other person see the world as you do, and try first to understand the world as they do. Why is it that they see the issue of gay marriage or affirmative action or abortion or Middle East policy so differently from you?

What helps most in these conversations is asking questions, and listening to the answer with an open mind. Turn your judgments into questions. Turn "You're wrong," into, "Why is it that you see it this way? Are you looking at different things? Do you know something I don't?" Having an open mind doesn't mean you have to agree with everything (or anything) someone else says; it means trying to understand before you judge. Too often we judge *before* we understand, and that just doesn't make sense.

3. Be Aware of Emotions

Emotions can be part of a constructive conversation. Feeling angry or hurt means you care—about the topic at hand and, often, about the other person. But emotions can keep us from listening to each other and cause us to say or do things we later regret. If you find yourself feeling upset, try to figure out why. Sometimes just saying that you're getting really upset by the conversation but aren't sure why can help move things forward. It can also make sense to take a break, especially if you're feeling overwhelmed. The conversation can wait.

Similarly, when the other person gets emotional, take it as a signal that the conversation has hit on something important that neither of you may fully understand. For example, when you say that "too few rich people care about poor people," the person you're talking with may feel anger welling up as they remember all the hardships their grandparents endured. They may feel stereotyped and misunderstood. The conversation seems to be about social policy, but to them it's also about the memory of their grandparents and the honor of their family. What might seem like an irrational outburst makes more sense when you understand what's behind it.

4. Give Each Other Space to Make Mistakes

If you're going to have a meaningful conversation about identity, you can pretty much assume that at some point someone is going to say something that hurts or offends the other. If people are not given the room to make a mistake or say something insensitive or hold a view that others find upsetting, then these conversations will be superficial, or they won't happen at all.

The advice here is twofold. On the one hand, remember that conversations about identity can cut to the core of who we are. You're entering territory where it's easy to hurt someone. Work hard to be sensitive to the well-being and concerns of the person you're talking with. If someone is upset, try to understand why. Take responsibility for what you've said and be willing to apologize.

On the other hand, be forgiving. Don't assume the other person is trying to upset you on purpose. Assume, at least at the outset, that a clumsy or thoughtless comment was made out of ignorance rather than malice. Describe your reaction without judging the other person. Instead of saying, "You're obviously a religious bigot," say, "It makes me angry that you think all Mormons have the same view on this."

Patience has its limits, of course. If someone continues to use language around you that you find abusive or offensive, then stop talking to them. If the situation persists, consider bringing the matter to the attention of an administrator or coach, or members of a relevant campus organization. No one should have to tolerate language or behavior that's offensive or bigoted or belittling.

5. Get Started Right

In some ways the toughest part of talking across differences is getting started. Some of the best conversations arise spontaneously, in the dining hall or during a study break. You don't have to worry about what to say, because by the time you realize what's going on, you're well into the conversation. But other conversations will start because *you* start them. There are better and worse ways to get things going.

When in doubt, ask. If you want to talk about something that you think might be offensive to someone, ask first. Instead of saying, "What race are you, anyway?!" you might say, "I tend to be interested in people's ethnic or racial backgrounds, and some people enjoy talking about that stuff, and some people don't. Is it something you're comfortable talking about?" They might just jump in and start, or they might hesitate. The important thing is to remember that it's up to them, and they don't have to explain their reasons.

Extend an invitation. If you're interested in talking with your roommate about your own sexual orientation, that's fine. If you're interested in talking to your roommate about your roommate's sexual orientation, and your roommate has never raised the issue, be careful. Don't go up to your roommate and say, "Hey, dude, are you gay? You can tell me." Even if your intentions are good, you might make your roommate uncomfortable, and you're unlikely to elicit a good conversation. Better, instead, to extend an invitation: "You and I never really talk about relationships and sex and things like that. I'm totally comfortable talking about that stuff. So, if you ever want someone to talk to, I just want you to know that I'm probably a good person for that."

Take the lead in being vulnerable. Nothing opens people up more quickly than when someone shares something important or makes themselves vulnerable in a way that, so far in the conversation, no one else has. You can wait for someone else to do that, or you can be the one who does it. In addition to stimulating a meaningful conversation, there's an added bonus: people are attracted to people who make themselves vulnerable. Those who take the risk are usually seen as being self-confident and secure in who they are.

THE JOURNEY'S THE THING

Instant Messenger

Craigster: Man, Mackie, I'm feeling a little lost. I'm a former pre-med, a former athlete, a former self-confident person.

Lil5Mackie: If your next sentence is "I'm the former boyfriend of Macani," I'm going to be really annoyed.

Craigster: Does every conversation have to be about you? Can't even my own feelings of being lost be about me and not you?

Lil5Mackie: Just trying to lighten the mood . . . which I guess I failed to do. I guess I'm a former funny person.

Craigster: Okay, that was at least sort of funny. But now back to me . . .

College is a great time for thinking about the big questions. But you can't find yourself just by thinking. You also have to *do.* Join groups, talk to people, explore new books and ideas, and most of all, stay engaged. Don't put your life on hold while you're waiting to find yourself. If you're thinking, "I'll really throw myself into something once I've figured out who I really am," you may be hindering your chances of finding what you're looking for. Ultimately, the "real you" isn't something you'll suddenly stumble upon, like buried treasure. The real you is the one doing the looking, and the deepest lessons are in the search itself.

6
Relationships

From: Rollo
To: Father O'Shea
Sent: Tuesday, November 9, 5:09 PM
Subject: My Soul

Dear Father O'Shea,

I write to inquire about how I might participate in a "confession." I am not Catholic, so I don't know what the sign-up procedures are. I would prefer a one-on-one session, but let me know what the group rate is as well.

The background is this: I am having "impure thoughts" about a girl in my chemistry class. Her name is Lauren, and she is the light of my life. In my youthful zeal to win Lauren's heart, I have begun to use cologne. My roommate says that women are defenseless against this particular odor. And now I am wracked with guilt. Is it fair to Lauren to use means of attraction that strip her of her free will?

To be clear, it doesn't seem to be working so far. And yet,

even as I know it's wrong, I continue to hope. Thanks for listening and I look forward to receiving your brochure.

Rollo

Ah, relationships. College students spend vast amounts of time trying to find their way into them and to wriggle their way out. Students talk endlessly with friends, lamenting the lack of someone special, and analyze every interaction and scrap of communication with a prospect for signs of possible romantic intent. Was that a smiley face in the e-mail, or just punctuation?

Pursuing a romantic possibility can bring out the best in us—we've never been smarter, funnier, or more energized. But it can also bring out our "not best." Should you really be flirting with your best friend's boyfriend? (Answer: no.) Did you actually press the Send button on that e-mail on purpose? Should you really have spilled your guts to the lady who checks the IDs at the dining hall?

Relax; you aren't the first to fumble your way through relationships in college and you won't be the last. The key is to be mindful about what you want and why, and to be willing to work through the tough parts.

INFATUATION AND THE UNREQUITED CRUSH

Quick quiz: How many songs can you think of with the word *love* in them? Did you guess *infinity*? Then you're on the right track. Love, someone once said, is a many-splendored thing. We don't know exactly what that means, but when you love someone who loves you back, it certainly *feels* many-splendored. Your stomach fills with butterflies, a silly smile is plastered on your face, and the world is a happy place. You could write a few song verses yourself.

But when the one you love does not return your affections, then love, well, stinks. Having an unrequited crush can feel like addiction withdrawal. You lose concentration and get less enjoyment out of things that used to make you happy. Your self-esteem plummets, and in extreme cases, you can even fall into a depression.

THE PERILS OF IDEALIZATION

Idealization is at the root of it all. It's love's way of grabbing you and keeping your attention focused on the object of your affection. Idealization turns that person who is pretty cool into a person who is perfect.

From: PJ
To: Macani
Sent: Thursday, January 27, 2:18 PM
Subject: FW: favor

Macani—this is a disaster! Just got this e-mail (see below) from a girl on my crew team!
>Hi PJ,
>Does Cube live upstairs from you? You totally have to introduce me to him.

>I've seen him a couple of times at the Weekly Spy office. He is so unbelievably hot,
>don't you think? And he is He-Larious! Maybe the funniest guy at the paper.
>And brilliant. I can't remember the last time I felt so excited about someone. Can
>you set up some scheme for hanging out with him, like a movie night or something?
>Thanks so much!
>Alpana

Macani, can you believe this?! Cube?! Maybe she's talking about a different Cube. There could be other Cubes, right? Should I tell her the truth about what he's really like? Or maybe she already knows the truth and has just lost her mind.

Please advise,
PJ

"Perfect," as you can see, means different things to different people. Some of us turn the other person into a god or goddess. We admire everything about them, and their mere presence elevates us. For others, "perfect" is about the other person being vulnerable and mixed up in just the right ways. We admire their authenticity, respond to their neediness; we want to take care of them and help them find meaning and joy. And for some, "perfect" is about just having fun together. Two people start out as best friends, and then one of them starts to see deeper possibilities.

When we're infatuated, we also idealize the way our life would be if the other person felt the way we feel. It would be beyond great, beyond fulfilling. It would fix everything about ourselves that we don't like, and make up for every mistake we've ever made.

But when the other person *doesn't* feel the way we feel . . .

Getting Over It

The unrequited crush can hit anyone, no matter how self-confident, popular, and socially adept. How to handle the disappointment? Here are a few tips.

It takes time. Your friends will tell you this, and when they say it, it will be annoying. But it's true. Feeling miserable and low is a normal reaction to rejection, and the feelings lift after a period of time. You can compare it in some ways to being physically sick. If you thought your flu would last forever, you'd be a lot more upset. But you know that you'll recover. The same is true for getting through emotional pain. Whether it lasts a week or a month, it will go away—and just knowing that can help speed up the healing.

See them as they really are. Working to unravel your idealized perceptions of your love object is no easy feat. It's not about tearing the person down; just don't build them up, and don't give them the benefit of every doubt. When they don't call when they said they would, the idealizing response is to make an excuse for them, or to blame yourself. "They're really busy with important things," we think, or, "It's because I wasn't interesting enough in that conversation after class."

But maybe what not calling really means is that the person can sometimes be inconsiderate or self-absorbed. Be willing to tell a new story about them—not a story that they're evil, but a story in which they are made of flesh and blood like everyone else. If you notice a pattern of making excuses for them, or blaming yourself for their shortcomings, stop.

Keep a healthy perspective on yourself. When someone you love doesn't love you back, it's hard not to take it as a referendum on your worth as a human being. You end up lying awake at night mulling over where exactly you fell short. If only you were taller or shorter, funnier, cooler, more generous, or better looking. Maybe you came on too strong, or not strongly enough. Maybe it was that stupid joke you made, or those shoes you wore.

Of course, these thoughts are ridiculous. Not that you aren't flawed: you are, but so is everyone else. If you had to be perfect to be loved, well, you see where that would go.

When the immediate pain of rejection starts to recede, you'll begin to see yourself more clearly again. To speed the process up a bit, try this: think of someone who knows and loves you—your grandmother, your best friend, your clarinet teacher, your dad. Then write a letter to yourself as if from one of them, listing the things they like best and appreciate about you.

It may feel a little strange at first, but try it. Why? Because it's hard for you to see your own best qualities right after you've been rejected. But it's not hard for others. They still see all the great things that make you you. If you're not in the mood to pretend to be someone else, then seek out the actual person and ask for a pep talk. Let them know that you don't want advice about what you did wrong or what you should do now. You just want to hear what they like about you. Hearing it said out loud will help silence some of your own negative thoughts and allow you to focus on all the good (and real) stuff again.

Stay active. No matter how brokenhearted you are, don't quit the hockey team and don't stop studying. When people are overwhelmed with emotional issues, playing on a team or studying can feel unimportant. It's easy to drop things altogether, figuring, "Well, who cares about that stupid class, anyway? All that matters is this other person."

But staying active can distract you from how you're feeling and give you something to feel good about. And whether or not studying makes you feel better, *not* studying will make you feel a whole lot worse. Getting over someone requires you to let the rest of your life back in, and keeping up with your studies and activities is a good place to start.

Of course, you're not a robot. If you find yourself in an incapacitating rut that just won't let up, it may be time to seek help. Getting back on your feet can be tough, and you don't have to go it alone. Take a look at Chapter 9 for ideas on how to make sure you get the help you need.

When the Attraction Is Mutual

Sometimes your interest in someone else is reciprocated. That, of course, is pretty great. Hard as it is to do, though, you have to keep good news in perspective as well, because that perfect being you're with at the beginning of a relationship will eventually turn back into a human being. Things that once seemed sexy or adorable may seem neutral or even annoying. Like that clucking noise they make when they eat. Why did *that* seem cute? Or the way they call their mother "mom" instead of "my mom." Don't they realize other people have mothers too?

But this is a good thing, not bad. The fact that you're not dating a god or goddess anymore isn't about them, it's about you. It means you've escaped from the clutches of infatuation and are free to have a real relationship with a real person.

E-MAIL AND IM: FLIRTING BETWEEN THE LINES

Can you tell when someone likes you and when they don't? Sometimes it's obvious, but just as often it's not. There's no announcement on the evening news, no big ad in the morning paper. All you have to go on is that awkward conversation after class, or that meal together that may or may not have "meant something."

E-mail and e-flirting can make things even less clear. You send off a note with just enough edge to keep things interesting, but not so much edge that you can't later say you were "just kidding." You not-so-secretly hope they'll respond in kind, and when they do, it makes your night. If they don't, you wonder whether you should have been more explicit.

It's easy to understand why students often prefer to flirt from the safety of their own keyboard. But e-mails and IMs can be hard to interpret, especially when you don't know the other person very well. They strip away information we typically rely on for deciphering meaning—tone, facial expression, body language. And so we're left filling in the blanks, a little like hearing someone tap out a rhythm and trying to figure out the corresponding tune.

Reading Messages

Below, Sweeney describes his exchange with a potential love interest to PJ.

Instant Messenger

Sweeneee: So I'm IM'ing this new chick Holly from psychology. And she says, and I quote, "Maybe you should come over and do the psych problem set with me. Ha ha." And then I get her away message, which is "Got the munchies."

PeaJ: "New chick?" I hate that phrase.

Sweeneee: That's not the point. The point is, not only did she invite me over, she invited me over to do a *psych* problem set. "Psychology" translates into "mind games" which translates into "I'm totally into you."

PeaJ: Maybe she actually needs help with psych, and is under the horribly mistaken notion that you could supply it. Or, wait, I know, she can tell from your comments in class that you don't actually know anything. Hence the "ha ha."

Sweeneee: So, she really is trying to invite me over?

PeaJ: Or maybe she could tell you were angling for an invite, and so she tried to get rid of you by offering the most unappealing invitation she could think of, and then left so you couldn't reply.

Sweeneee: Yeah, why did she leave right after? I'm thinking maybe she went to talk about me with her friend.

PeaJ: Maybe someone got onto her IM and was pretending to flirt with you.

Sweeneee: I'm not liking the direction your theories are going. Maybe I'll just go over anyway.

Sweeney certainly has his own special way of interpreting this exchange, and that's just the point. E-mail and IM leave room for creative interpretations, and it's a practice we all engage in. How to avoid straying too far afield?

Calm down. Remember, the relationship is not going to hinge on your ability to interpret one unclear e-mail. Anyone who likes you is going to like you whether or not you get their "secret" message and respond in just the right way.

Check the context. It's tempting to take a phrase and analyze it to death: "Why did he write 'see ya' instead of 'see you'?" "What was she getting at when she wrote 'I'll talk to you tomorrow'?" Odds are, the message is in line with your general relationship. If you're thinking, "She's never shown any romantic interest in me, but I think that reference to her problem set might mean she wants to sleep with me," you're probably a little wide of the mark.

Make sure they understood your prior message. Sometimes messages that seem random or confusing are the result of the other person misinterpreting a previous message from you. Go back and look at what you wrote, and see if you can reinterpret your e-mail in a way that makes theirs easier to understand.

Just ask. Regardless of what you ultimately decide the message means, remember that, at best, it's an educated guess. In your reply, leave open the possibility that you're mistaken. Better yet, share your theory ("Hey, my problem set and I are happy to pay a visit") and then check it out ("Or were you just kidding about me coming over? I wasn't sure.").

PJ caught Sweeney on IM the next day to catch up on what had happened.

Instant Messenger

PeaJ: Did you actually go over to Holly's place last night? You weren't in your room.

Sweeneee: Yeah, yeah, just stopped over. She and a bunch of her friends were eating pizza in the common room.

PeaJ: Wow! I can't believe you got away with just showing up there.

Sweeneee: You mis-underestimate me, madam. She even agreed to out to the movies with me . . . along with her friends.

PeaJ: Well, there you go. "New chick" comes through.

Writing Messages

Even more important than how you interpret messages is how you write them.

Remember, they'll assume the worst. Because it's sometimes hard to interpret emotion, humor, and overall tone in writing, proofread your messages with an eye toward what might be misunderstood. For example, if you write, "Why didn't you write me sooner?!!" it could mean, "You're an inconsiderate jerk!" or it could mean, "I missed you. I'm so excited to hear from you." So give some extra thought to how you put things, especially if the message is important or if the message has some emotional content.

Avoid T. U. I. (typing under the influence). There are the usual kinds of influences: alcohol, anger, sleep deprivation. If you're under the influence of any of these, best not to press the Send button until the next morning, or at least until a trusted friend has looked over the message.

Infatuation is another influence to watch out for. Infatuation has a way of slowing down time. Minutes take hours, hours take days, and the idea of waiting until morning is excruciating. Everything feels like an emergency and must be figured out *this second*, even if this second happens to be 3:00 a.m.

But the rule still holds (and still rhymes): wait to send or ask a friend. Say this to yourself: "It seems like a good idea to send this. In fact, it seems like the very survival of humankind is at stake. But I know that's just an illusion due to my cloudy state of mind. So I'll just wait until tomorrow to figure it all out." If, the next day, it still makes sense, go ahead and send it. Otherwise, let it be your little secret.

ARE YOU PLAYING BY THE SAME RULES?

Here's another quiz: read this e-mail from Sweeney to Duncan, and then answer the question that follows it.

From: Sweeney
To: Duncan
Sent: Thursday, January 27, 2:18 PM
Subject: overreacting?

Hey Dunk,

Glad you liked the picture I sent. I agree, Holly is the hottest girl I've ever dated. Second prize is not even being awarded.

But that's also a problem. Half the guys on campus are in love with her, and I wouldn't say she minds the attention. She's gonna end up being the social chair at her sorority, which means, well, I don't know what it means. She'd never admit it, but what it really comes down to is that I'm her boyfriend when she feels like it. So it's great, horrible, great, horrible. If I wasn't so into her, I'd just say forget it. But it's Holly.

Sweeney

Based on this e-mail, which best describes the situation between Sweeney and Holly?

(a) Holly is taking advantage of Sweeney. She's using him when she feels lonely, but has no real interest in him.
(b) Holly really likes going out with Sweeney, but doesn't want to be exclusive with him.
(c) Holly loves Sweeney and is totally faithful to him. She doesn't understand why Sweeney gets so jealous.

The correct answer is: we have no idea. And the trouble is, neither does Sweeney. Of course, he thinks the answer is (a). But he and Holly haven't discussed any of this. So we—and Sweeney—don't know what's going on from Holly's point of view, which means we can't really know what's going on with the relationship either.

In every relationship, there's a certain level of commitment involved, ranging from totally uncommitted to married. We each have assumptions about how serious things are, whether we can see other people, and how often we should hang out together. The problem comes when we each want different things and don't know how to talk about it.

How to Talk About Expectations

To be sure, talking about expectations is high stakes. We're afraid of what we might hear, or of what we'll have to say. So we often choose to keep things unclear, figuring that unclear is at least better than clear and bad.

But not talking about something doesn't make it go away. Incidents accumulate, people feel jealous or smothered, and eventually the relationship can quietly unravel. For his part, Sweeney will be miserable until he talks with Holly about what they each expect from the relationship—for better or for worse.

What helps?

Know yourself. All the talking in the world isn't going to help a relationship if you haven't first done some thinking about what you want and why. What level of commitment is best for you? What makes you feel secure? Are there certain behaviors that you find particularly upsetting? How do past experiences impact what's important to you (for example, your parents' divorce or a painful former relationship)? The more you've thought these issues through, the more clearly you can explain to someone else how you feel and what you want.

Be direct. Say what you want and why. The easiest way for the other person to know how you feel and what you want is for you to tell them. Don't assume they know, and don't make them guess.

If you get upset when your boyfriend says he'll call you but doesn't, tell him. Don't say, "I thought you were gonna call last night, but anyway, no big deal." Be explicit: "It's important to me that you call when you say you will. If you're not sure, just say so." And then say why: "When you say you'll call and then don't, I end up waiting around, and it makes me wonder if I'm that important to you."

If these words don't sound like you, find words that do. And if the issue is important to you, don't be afraid to say so. In fact, the words "this is important to me" are good ones to use. If you don't say it matters, the other person might assume it doesn't.

Ask what they want and why. Be clear up front that how the other person sees things matters to you. The best way to do that is by asking questions, even if you disagree with their view. If your boyfriend says he feels smothered by having to worry about whether he calls you every single time he says he will, don't respond with an attack. Don't say, "Is it really that difficult!?" or, "You're just making excuses!"

Instead, try to understand what he cares about, try to get inside what matters to him. You may or may not be able to come up with a "solution," but listening to his point of view and the feelings behind the words is one of the best ways to show you really care. There's little you can say that will matter as much.

Does all this talk about talk mean that you're supposed to have some big conversation every time one of you has a passing concern? Definitely not. There's a balance to be struck. Talk about what matters when it matters, but keep things in perspective. If you focus too much on *whether* a relationship is good, you may forget to have fun together, and that's the thing that *makes* a relationship good.

"I LOVE YOU" IS A CONVERSATION

There are two kinds of people: those who can say "I love you" and those who can't. What happens when these two kinds of people date each other?

Instant Messenger

Lil5Mackie: You know how just before we hang up I say "I love you" and you say "Yeah, bye." How come you don't say it back?

Craigster: Mackie, come on. You know I love you.

Lil5Mackie: Then say it.

Craigster: I just did.

Lil5Mackie: No, you said, "You know I love you." That's different. You're talking about what I know, not how you feel.

Craigster: Okay, Mackie, that's a little crazy. How do I feel? I feel in love with you.

Lil5Mackie: Then say it.

Craigster: I just did!! Twice!

Lil5Mackie: Just say, "Macani, I love you."

Craigster: I do.

Lil5Mackie: But you can't say it.

Craigster: Macani, I totally totally totally love you.

Lil5Mackie: Now take out the totally parts.

Craigster: Okay, I changed my mind. I used to love you until about thirty seconds ago.

Whether or not you're comfortable talking about feelings doesn't depend on being a guy. Different people just have different reactions to putting their emotions on the table.

It's easy to get our signals crossed. Most of us assume other people are just like us. If they're not saying "I love you," it's not because they find it hard to say. It's because they just don't care.

Sometimes that's true; often it's not. There are a lot of reasons someone might be reluctant to discuss feelings, first among them being vulnerability. When I say "I love you," I'm giving you the power to hurt me. If I've been wounded before, I may be particularly careful. I might not say "I love you" until a deeper level of trust has developed. Another reason has to do with meaning. Some people equate affection with commitment and have a high threshold for what constitutes love. They treat love like a scarce resource that has to be parceled out with great care.

The conversation itself can feel like a bind. Saying "I love you" is a statement, but it's also an implicit question: "Do you love me?" The conversation is like a high-stakes knock-knock joke. When you say "Knock, knock," the other person knows that anything other than "Who's there?" is the wrong answer. Even if the other person does love you, they might resent feeling pressured to say so.

What to do? Make "I love you" a conversation. Instead of hoping they say it back and feeling resentful if they don't, talk about it directly: "I can't always tell how you feel about me. Is that something you feel comfortable talking about?" Tell them why it's hard for you when they don't express affection, and let them know what you want. If they're uncomfortable talking about this stuff, don't say, "Well, that's a terrible way to be." Instead, ask them why it's hard for them. Whether or not they're good at expressing themselves, remember that their point of view matters as much as yours.

Instant Messenger

Craigster: So, I just don't understand why it matters so much if I say it. I mean, I do love you, you know I love you, I know you know, so what are we talking about here?

Lil5Mackie: Well, I guess I need reassurance.

Craigster: I don't know. That's not my thing. Isn't it enough that we just know we love each other and leave it at that?

Lil5Mackie: Maybe when we were together. But now that we're so far away, it's like I really need to know that you care. How am I supposed to know that you're not losing interest in me, or running off with someone else?

Craigster: Mackie, I've always been honest with you. I'll always be honest with you. You know that, right?

Lil5Mackie: I know. And I appreciate that. And I want to be honest with you, which is why I even bothered to bring this up.

Craigster: Yeah, I know. I guess it's just that my parents always used to say "I love you" to each other like every five seconds. And you know what? They didn't love each other even a little. Instead of going around telling everyone about it, I wish they had just tried to get along a little better.

Lil5Mackie: I know. I guess our parents are really different. My parents say it too, but they really do love each other.

This is the beginning of an important conversation. Like other serious relationship talks, how it comes out matters less than how it's conducted. Talking openly and listening with generosity are going to be a good thing no matter what.

THE LONG-DISTANCE CHALLENGE

Long-distance relationships create their own special challenges, physical distance being only the most obvious. It's just plain hard to be in a relationship when you can't spend much time together.

It's especially tough since college is a time of so much change. One of you might change more than the other, or begin to move in a direction that the other doesn't understand. And that can create more than just physical distance.

Then there's the temptation of all the people around you. You meet someone you like, but they know you're already taken. You become closer and closer, but you're careful to stay faithful to your boyfriend or girlfriend at home. But when things get rocky between you and your long-distance beau, who are you going to turn to? Despite your best intentions, the new friendship starts to feel intimate.

That's not to say that long-distance relationships can't work. They can and do. But they require even more trust and clarity of commitment than other relationships. The commitment is not just to each other, but to the situation. You have to be committed to working through the inevitable jealousies and misunderstandings that come up. If the trust and commitment aren't there, it's just not going to work.

Long-distance relationships do have one thing going for them: absence, as they say, makes the heart grow fonder. However, a word of caution for when you finally get to be together: your expectations might be unrealistically high from the anticipation and idealization that built up during the separation. Expect some relationship jet lag; it can take time to get used to being back together.

THE PERILS OF CHEATING

No matter how solid your current relationship, there can be temptations to cheat. No one's perfect, and it's not our role to come down on you for fooling around with someone while you're dating someone else. But we will share an observation: cheating ends up making people miserable. It sets off a storm of jealousy, anger, and guilt, and the damage you do to your relationship will likely be terminal.

If you *want* to break up with the person you're currently seeing, don't use cheating as a way to do it. It might seem like an easy way out ("Once he finds out, *he'll* break up with *me*"), but it's not. Keep things clean; end your current relationship before seeing someone new.

Remember, when you fool around behind someone's back, you're sending the new person a message about you. You might think the message is, "I'm so attracted to you that I simply can't wait any longer," but the real message has to do with trust: "If you and I do end up dating, you won't be able to trust that I'll be faithful." If the new relationship has promise, it can wait.

PHYSICAL AND EMOTIONAL ABUSE

No relationship will make you happy every second of the day, and no relationship is without the occasional misunderstandings, disappointments, and hard feelings.

But physical and emotional abuse are different. These are lines that should never be crossed, or even approached. *Any* form of physical violence is unacceptable (and illegal). No one should ever hit you, slap you, push you, or threaten you. That goes for women and men. There's no acceptable excuse, no provocation that justifies it. No matter how sorry the person seems afterward, make sure you get whatever assistance and support you need. If you want to stay in the relationship, do it *only after* the other person gets professional help.

Emotional abuse is more complicated, though if you're asking yourself if there's been emotional abuse in your relationship, that's a pretty good indication that something's wrong. Here are examples of some warning signs. The person you're dating:

- says to you, "It's lucky I'm going out with you because no one else ever would."
- cheats on you, promises to change, then cheats again.
- is nice to you in private but nasty to you in public, or vice versa.
- uses anger or the threat of leaving to get their way.

The bottom line is this: what matters is how *you* feel. If the relationship causes you to feel worse about yourself rather than better, or creates emotional havoc in your life rather than stability, then it doesn't matter what you call the problem. It's enough that you see that there is one.

BREAKING UP

Cheating and abuse may be the most dramatic reasons relationships end, but they are not the only ones. You want time off or more freedom, or maybe it just wasn't the right match. Figuring out whether to stay or go can be gut-wrenching, and whichever side of the breakup you're on, you're in for a bumpy ride.

When You End the Relationship

One of the hardest things about breaking up is telling the other person it's over. You desperately want the other person to feel okay about being dumped, but there's nothing you can

say or do that helps. If you've ever been rejected, you know
the feeling.

From: PJ
To: Macani
Sent: Wednesday, April 20, 11:39 PM
Subject: dumpster

Hey, Macani,

I need some heavy-duty relationship advice—I think I'm going
to break up with Abby. Oh, you BETTER not be laughing,
because this is making me ill!! Yes, you're allowed to say I told
you so.
 Anyway, it never occurred to me how crappy being on this
side of it would feel. I still really care about Abby, and I just
can't bear the idea of hurting her. Just thinking about it
makes me feel like such a bad person. I wish she would break
up with me.

PJ

PJ's feelings are common, and in fact, it would be strange
if PJ wasn't upset by the idea of hurting Abby. Still, you can't
stay in a relationship just because you don't want the other
person to get hurt.

Your goal can't be for the other person not to feel upset.
They will be. Your goal instead is to handle your side of the
conversation with some grace. That means being kind and caring, but also clear. If you've made up your mind to end things,

make sure that comes across. Leaving the other person with false hope can seem like a generous thing to do, but it's not.

Being clear *doesn't* mean you have to be brutally honest. If the other person begs to know exactly why you're breaking up, you don't need to say, "Because you're boring" or, "Because I met someone much more attractive and exciting." Keep the reasons honest, but skip the details: "I just haven't been that happy" or "I still want to see other people." People *say* they want specifics, but they don't.

When You Get Dumped

From: Sweeney
To: Duncan
Sent: Friday, April 29, 9:09 PM
Subject: D-Day

Having a bad day, Dunk. Holly just came by and told me it's over. Worst I've ever felt in my life. Ever. Call me.

Sweeney

Few things in the normal course of life are as painful as being dumped. You're losing companionship and intimacy, your self-esteem can be affected, and your sense of the future has to be rebuilt from the ground up. If any of this sounds familiar, it's because being dumped creates the same emotional disturbances as the unrequited crush. Of course, in this case, you've *had* a relationship, and that's something the person with a crush would love to have experienced. If you asked them, they'd say, "If I could just date that person for a week, I'd be happy. I promise that if they break up with me, I won't complain."

But people don't make good on that promise. If they still like the other person, they feel miserable when the breakup comes. It's better to have loved and lost than never to have loved at all. But don't tell that to someone too soon after a relationship has ended. They're going to feel miserable, and, as we said about the unrequited crush, getting over it is going to take time.

Rollo Spencer, Rm. 6

Dear Fellow First-Floor Dwellers,
    I would like to explain the events of yesterday evening. I certainly did not anticipate that when I invited my lady friend Lauren Katchor over to see my Lego tribute to Elvis, my roommate would run up and down the hall banging on your doors yelling, "Hey everybody, Rollo's getting some!"
    I must admit that I had hoped some sort of romantic relationship between Miss Katchor and myself was in the offing, but sadly, when she heard Sweeney's rantings, she vanished forthwith from my room and, I expect, from my life.
    Thanks to those of you who commented on how attractive she was. And for those of you who were duly upset at being woken up, rest assured that there is no risk of any woman ever accepting an invitation to my room again.
    Do give Sweeney my best. That he has destroyed the culminating moment of my teenage years is not entirely his fault. Should not his parents bear some culpability for these sad events?

Best,
Rollo

Sex can be exciting, fulfilling, and fun, and we're guessing this isn't the first time you've heard that. You've probably also heard a lot about the "other side" of sex—about pregnancy, disease, acquaintance rape, and the complex impact sex can have on relationships and identity.

This chapter is about all of those things. Some of it may be familiar, but we also discuss issues that get less airtime. In addition to the information toward the end of the chapter on pregnancy, contraception, and health, we look at sex and identity, and the challenges of talking about physical intimacy with a boyfriend or girlfriend.

SEXUAL EXPERIENCES AND HOW WE TALK ABOUT THEM

Most people don't talk all that openly about their sex lives or lack thereof. Sure, there's the occasional game of Truth or Dare, or Your Most Embarrassing Moment, but such confessions tend to sound a little self-promoting: "My most embarrassing moment was when I was making out with this international supermodel, when all of sudden this other international supermodel walked in on us without knocking!" Talk about embarrassing.

What We Don't Say

And how about when you first meet someone in college? You might say, "Hi, where are you from?" or, "Hi, what are you majoring in?" No one says, "Hi, I'm a virgin. I sometimes worry that I'll never have sex. I'm not even sure I masturbate properly." You *might* talk about some of that stuff later in a friendship, but even then, only with someone you know really well.

From: Macani
To: PJ
Sent: Friday, October 15, 7:14 PM
Subject: Sex Tips from Macani

Hey, Peej, I just had this crazy conversation. You know Katelyn, of Katelyn and Luke? So I'm at the Friday on the Green concert, and she comes over to me, and we start talking about her relationship with Luke, which was interesting, but then the next thing you know she's asking for my advice about her sex life (!), as if I have any idea what I'm talking about!! So I told her that "it comes down to timing," which I thought was pretty quick thinking, but then for some reason I added, "Timing, that is, with a small 't,'" and she was all, "Oh, totally with a small 't.'"

Anyway, in order to avoid ever seeing her again, I may have to transfer.

Macani

In social settings, there's pressure to sound like one of the gang. When the topic turns to boyfriends from high school, you don't want to be the only one to say that you didn't have one. So you turn "Tony, the neighbor I went to my prom with," into "Tony, my boyfriend." While others talk excitedly about "first experiences," you stay quiet about the fact that your own first experiences were emotional and a little scary, or that you haven't *had* any first experiences. When it comes to talking about sex, it can feel like everyone else is more experienced and less confused.

Talking about sex is a good example of the Inside-Out Trap at work (see Chapter 2). The people who are inexperienced or feel confused are less likely to speak up, and the people who do talk try to make their stories sound like everyone else's.

"Am I the Only One Who Hasn't Had Sex?"

Tons of college students haven't had sex. For some, abstinence is a religious matter. Others are waiting for the right person, or don't feel ready yet. Concerns about pregnancy and disease are also a big factor. And some people simply aren't that interested.

Of course, there are also a lot of students who want to have sex but haven't. Now, you may be thinking, "True enough, but I'm beyond inexperienced. I haven't even kissed anyone. I've never even been on a date." That too describes a larger number of your classmates than you might guess, though the perception is otherwise.

Part of the concern about experience is practical. "Am I falling behind? How will the other person react if they realize I've never done this?" Remember, there's a decent chance that when the time comes, the person you're with will be similarly inexperienced, and worrying about how *you'll* react to *them*.

Regardless, the truth is that "experience" matters to virtually no one. If you were attracted to someone, would you care that they didn't have much experience fooling around? Learning to kiss takes about four seconds; for anything else, the person you're with will be happy to show you what they know, and the two of you can figure out the rest together.

The whole question of "will I be good at this" starts from a flawed premise. Sex isn't math. It isn't about getting it "right," or learning some set of secret techniques that only the cool people know. It's about learning what you each like, and even for experienced people, that can involve a bunch of fumbling around.

SEX AND COMMUNICATION (OR, "WHAT'S WRONG WITH YOU?")

Talking about the physical side of relationships can be difficult and complicated, even for people who are normally good communicators, and even when two people really care about each other.

When Craig visits Macani at school for the first time in November, they experience these difficulties firsthand. Macani describes to PJ what happened.

From: Macani
To: PJ
Sent: Sunday, November 7, 2:25 PM
Subject: blah

Thanks for staying at your mom's last night. You asked how it went. Umm . . . horrible?

Craig and I were fooling around, nothing too out of the ordinary, except that we were in my bed, which, where else can we be in our room, right? But then he starts pushing things further than in the past. And so I told him we should stop because I was feeling uncomfortable.

And so he gives me this look and is like, "Fine, I'll sleep on the floor." So I said, "Am I supposed to do something I don't want to?" And he's like, "Come on, Macani. We've been going out for a year! We're in college." So I was like, "So what? Is the only reason you came up here to have sex!?"

So, stupid idiot that I am, I ended up feeling guilty that Craig was sleeping on the floor and told him he could sleep in the bed with me. So he comes back into the bed, but then he starts trying to fool around again, which really upset me, so I said we shouldn't, and he's like, "Forget this," and went back to the floor.

And this morning he's acting like everything is fine and normal, like there was no problem at all.

PJ, I'm so stressed about this. Maybe I don't understand the rules. Am I being a bad girlfriend? I just don't get why Craig, who is usually so nice, would care so little about making me feel so bad.

Mac

After a few hours, Macani sends a similar e-mail to Craig, and Craig writes back:

From: Craig
To: Macani
Sent: Sunday, November 7, 6:49 PM
Subject: stuff

Hey Macani,

We should definitely talk on the phone. I can tell you're really upset. To be honest, me too, especially because of what you said about the only reason I was visiting was to have sex. You know that is so not true so I don't understand why you would say that.

I've always respected that you didn't want to go all the way, and I've tried hard not to make it a big deal, even though for me it kind of is. But the way we were talking about my visit and PJ staying away, I wondered if you wanted to go further than we have in the past (and since you always want me to be honest with you, I admit that I was hoping you did).

So, when we were fooling around and you wanted to stop, I was like, okay, that's fine, I can sleep on the floor.

But then you wanted me to come back to the bed, and looked like you were going to cry and everything, so I did. And when we started to fool around again you seemed as into it as I was! And then you said to stop again, so then I was like, okay this is making me crazy, I'm just gonna sleep on the floor. Isn't that the right thing to do?

This morning I was trying to say everything is still cool between us, and so I said I love you. But I'm sorry if you thought that was the wrong thing.

Craig

People's reactions to the two e-mails will depend on their own life experiences and views and, to some extent, on how they are telling the story to themselves of what happened between Craig and Macani. What we know for sure is that they're both upset, and that alone is enough to tell us that something has gone wrong.

Different Experiences

Let's start with the obvious though important observation that Macani and Craig each had very different experiences of their own and each other's behaviors. Let's consider how each might have been thinking about the situation, specifically about the issue of Craig sleeping on the floor.

Macani's thoughts. This is what was going through Macani's mind: "When Craig said he would sleep on the floor, it was like him saying, 'If you won't fool around, fine. Then I don't love you and don't want to be with you.' That broke my heart. We hadn't seen each other in months, and I was feeling so vulnerable already and I just needed to know he still cared about me. I wanted him to come back to the bed, and I said, 'Can't we just hug?' but when he came back into the bed he starting pressuring me again, which he's never done before, and that just made everything worse."

Craig's thoughts. Meanwhile, Craig was thinking this: "When Macani said she didn't want to keep fooling around, I got really depressed because I was thinking maybe she wasn't attracted to me or wasn't into me anymore. I'd been looking forward to seeing her for so long. I was getting really sexually frustrated, so I thought it made the most sense to sleep on the floor. When she asked me to come back, I said no, but she really wanted me to, so I did. We started hugging and fooling around, and I was thinking she was feeling more comfortable, but then she wanted to stop again. So I just ended up really confused about what was going on and how she felt about me.".

Macani and Craig were each contending with a lot of un-expressed thoughts and feelings that night. Each ends up mis-understanding what was going on for the other, and why they did what they did. The more upset people feel, the more likely they are to get their signals crossed in ways that hurt the other and damage or ruin the relationship.

Different Tendencies

Another factor in what's going on may relate to the not-so-simple differences between men and women. Talking about these differences runs the risk of perpetuating the danger-ously wrongheaded notion that "boys will be boys" and aren't responsible for their own behavior. On the other hand, insist-ing that there are no differences between men and women runs the risk of ignoring important factors that can contribute to conflict, and to the pain and trauma that result.

Recognizing that what follows are generalizations, and that many men and women don't conform to these observa-tions, we offer some thoughts for women, followed by some thoughts for men.

For women: why guys can seem like jerks. Let's be clear: some guys *are* jerks. Of course, most aren't (we don't know the exact numbers). For many guys, when they get sex-ually excited, it can be hard for them to focus on anything else. And "being sexually excited" isn't something that is lim-ited to the time just before and during whatever fooling around goes on. Women are sometimes surprised to hear that on a date that involved dinner, a movie, and then a kiss at the end of the night, the guy was spending the whole four hours prior to the kiss thinking about sex.

The more a guy wants to have sex, the worse he becomes at reading signals that are anything other than blatant. When you say no, but continue to kiss him, he's thinking, "Well, she's slowly coming around." He's trying to do to you what he would want you to do to him: "If I get her in the mood, she'll want to keep doing this."

He may not understand the complexity of how you're feeling. He may not be getting all the layers of where you're really at: "I really care about you. I'm just not sure I want to do this right now. I wish you would give me more space and time for me to figure out how I feel. I like the physical intimacy, but I really resent being pushed, and that's making me want to push you away. But I don't want you to feel hurt," and so forth.

What he nets from your words and actions is either "Yes, we're fooling around, so everything is great" or "No sex tonight. I reject you." Or, if he's more clued in than most, he might understand that you're feeling ambivalent, but get the wrong idea about what that means. He thinks you're saying: "I don't know what I want so keep trying to persuade me."

This is not to say that men don't have similar ambivalences about what is going on. It's just that while women tend to confront those ambivalences before and while they're fooling around, men are more likely to think, "Let's keep going and worry about everything else later."

All of which conspires to make communication extremely difficult. It's made even more complicated by the fact that you don't want to hurt the guy's feelings, and you want him to still like you. And yet, if you are to be clear, you have to hit him over the head with the fact that you do *not* want to have sex or fool around further.

For guys: what's up with her? The key thing for guys to understand is that some women have a harder time than you do in saying what they do and don't want. Guys often think, "If I want to have sex, I'll say so, either in words or actions. If I don't want to, I'll say so. I assume she'll do the same." Sometimes that's true for women, but sometimes it's not. It's important for guys to understand the reasons women can feel conflicted.

Some women feel unsure if they're "allowed" to stop once they've started. A woman may know intellectually that she has the right to stop whenever she wants and that consent can be revoked at any time, but she may still feel confused by some notion that once things have gotten going, it's somehow not fair to the guy if she chooses to stop. The guy may seem upset when she indicates that she doesn't want to fool around, and she feels upset that the guy is upset. She assumes that the only way to help the guy to not be upset is to continue down the path of increased physical intimacy.

In addition, a woman may have unresolved conflicts within herself. Do I really want to do this? How will I feel in the morning? She's asking herself tonight all the questions you'll be asking yourself tomorrow. You'll jump off the cliff and, only once you're halfway down, try to determine whether that was such a good idea. She's trying to do the reasonable thing and figure out whether it's such a good idea before she jumps.

On top of all that, she's trying to deal with you the whole time. She's evaluating your behavior as you fool around. Is he being respectful of where I'm at? Are we going at the right speed? Am I comfortable with this? You may be focusing on the fact that you're getting sexually frustrated, and try to push things ahead. But you're probably underestimating how upsetting it can be for her to feel pushed faster than she wants to go. The harder you push, the more likely she is to feel upset, and the less likely she is to feel comfortable continuing.

Related to that, the woman probably wants you to like her. She wants to stay friends or continue to date, even if she wants the physical side of things to go more slowly. She's not sure if you're okay with that and may be afraid that you won't want to see her again.

A final factor is fear. Most likely, you are physically stronger than the woman you are fooling around with. Even if she trusts you, it can feel enormously threatening to a woman when she feels she is saying no and you are continuing to push. Things can go from feeling safe to feeling unsafe in a flash. And, of course, the fear she feels only makes it more difficult for her to be clear.

The Bottom Line on Communication

That's a lot of complex stuff to keep in mind. Of course, the best advice is to discuss everything in advance. But sometimes people feel confused in the middle of fooling around, and for those times, we distill a few bedrock principles.

If the other person indicates any hesitation, stop. Don't assume the problem is that they're just a little nervous, or need to be warmed up, or that you can change their mind by getting further into it. Disengage and ask, "Is this okay? How are you feeling? How are you doing with this?" If the answer is anything other than, "This is great. Let's keep going," then *stop*. Reassure them that stopping is fine, and that it won't affect the relationship.

If you feel hesitant, disengage. Either one of you is allowed to stop *at any point*. There's no point after which it's too late, regardless of what the other person says or how they act.

Disengage physically and be explicit (you can say, "Stop; I'm uncomfortable; don't do that"). Don't worry that this will hurt the other person's feelings or make them not like you. Your consent and safety are more important. You can figure out the relationship issues later.

If you're going to have intercourse, talk first. Before having intercourse, certain conversations are *required*. Of course, the first issue is consent. Do you each agree that you want to have sex? Consent must always be explicit and unambiguous. Then, you not only have to figure out what method of contraception to use, but discuss what you'll do if a pregnancy results. You should talk about past sexual history and whether you've been tested for sexually transmitted diseases and AIDS.

If you're thinking, "Well, those conversations are too scary and serious," then you shouldn't be having sex. And if you're thinking, "Those conversations will kill the moment," that's the point. Sex isn't just about the moment. It can change the course of your entire life.

A WORD ON HOOKING UP

You're probably familiar with the phrase "hooking up," but you may not know precisely what it means. Here's how PJ and Sweeney discuss the question when it comes up in conversation late one night:

PJ: I think the technical definition is that "hooking up" is a casual romantic encounter between two friends, or maybe it's two acquaintances. Actually, maybe it's two strangers.

Sweeney: I thought it just meant you have sex with someone at 3:00 a.m.

PJ: No, it's not sex! It's just fooling around.

Sweeney: No, I'm pretty sure it means having sex.

PJ: Well, what does having sex mean, then?

Sweeney: Uh-oh.

PJ: Well, maybe the phrase is vague on purpose so that people don't have to mean anything specific when they say it.

Sweeney: I thought the whole purpose of talking with words was that they have a specific meaning.

PJ: So then what does "hooking up" mean?

For our purposes, we'll just assume it involves a physical encounter—some level of fooling around—with a person you aren't dating, at least not yet.

The Three Yeses

Obviously, the less well you know someone, the more likely it is that fooling around with them is going to create or contribute to problems (like the communication issues discussed above, or problems with consent or alcohol as discussed below).

If you are considering fooling around with someone at a party, here's something else to keep in mind. There are really *three* people who have to say yes before you consider hooking up—the Other Person; You Tonight; and You Tomorrow.

You Tonight might be all in favor. That's fine. That's one vote. But what about You Tomorrow? Will You Tomorrow feel lonely and upset? Taken advantage of or worried about sexually transmitted diseases? You Tonight might be saying, "Sure, a casual thing is fine," whereas You Tomorrow might end up thinking, "No, it's not. I was deceiving myself. If it's not going to turn into something, I shouldn't do it."

And how about the Other Person—do they know that you consider this a casual thing? It can be really hurtful for someone to find themselves abandoned by a person they thought was genuinely interested in a relationship with them. You might think, "Well, this is a party, of course they know it's casual." But college students don't share a common set of assumptions about the rules of the game, so you can't just make that assumption.

If you have a pattern of hooking up with people and being unhappy the next day, it's worth taking a hard look at why. You may be missing a very important yes.

MASTURBATION AND YOU

Instant Messenger

Sweeneee: Hey Peej, Rollo said that Women on Top is having a sex toy workshop tonight. Is that for real?

Peaj: Yeah, it's totally for real. I've been helping with planning. We're bringing in some experts to educate students about their options, pleasure-wise.

Sweeneee: Damn, that is cool! Can I come?

Peaj: I think it's girls only. It's about, you know, um, self-pleasure.

Sweeneee: This keeps getting better. Can you make an exception for me?

Peaj: It's not like it's going to be some wet T-shirt contest or, like, a Hollywood-style lesbian make-out session.

Sweeneee: Hey, I just want to be the enlightened 21st-century man.

PeaJ: Nice try, Sweeney. Look, if I learn anything interesting, I'll fill you in. And Rollo too.

Masturbating reduces the need and urgency for sex, with none of the risks of actual sex. Even masturbation in the context of a relationship can be a good fix if one person wants to fool around and the other doesn't. And in case you haven't been officially notified, no one goes blind from masturbating, and, in fact, only rarely is anyone injured.

Bottom line: masturbation is nothing to be embarrassed about. It serves a lot of useful purposes, and if you masturbate, you're in good company (so to speak).

STDS, CONTRACEPTION, AND PREGNANCY

If you plan on having sex, it's important to talk about sexual history, sexually transmitted diseases (STDs), contraception, and issues around pregnancy.

Sexually Transmitted Diseases

You should fully inform yourself about sexually transmitted diseases, whether it's from talking to someone at health services, attending an outreach session during freshman orientation, or doing Web research. STDs are actually quite common on college campuses, and contrary to those graphic slide shows that you may have seen in junior high school, many have only periodic symptoms or no symptoms at all.

The human papillomavirus (HPV), for example, is symptomless. Both men and women can transmit the disease, and it's a precursor to cervical cancer in women. Women are tested for the virus with a Pap smear and can be treated for it.

Another example is herpes. If you have herpes, it shows up in the form of periodic outbreaks. People who have herpes can transmit it to someone else even when they don't have any symptoms. Condoms help prevent transmission but don't protect entirely.

Women get tested for STDs more often than men because they go to see a doctor to get contraceptives. But it's everyone's responsibility to get tested. If you're a guy, that means you may need to make a special appointment. More often than not, STDs get passed along because someone didn't realize they had one. But that's no excuse.

HIV/AIDS. Everyone has heard of HIV/AIDS, but not everyone knows all they should about the disease. Some college students look around their school and see healthy, vital students and end up thinking to themselves, "I doubt anyone at my school has AIDS." But fully one-third of the people who have AIDS *don't know they have it.* Symptoms may not show up for many years, and people are contagious even before they have symptoms.

There are populations considered "high-risk," like gay men, intravenous drug users, prostitutes, or anyone who has had sex with someone in a high-risk group. But *anyone* can get AIDS from anyone who has it. That includes men and women of every age, sexual orientation, social class, and ethnic group. You can get AIDS from anal or vaginal intercourse, as well as from oral sex (it is transmitted through contact with blood, semen, vaginal fluid, and breast milk). Kissing is generally considered safe, though experts at the Centers for Disease Control caution against prolonged kissing with an infected partner, especially if you have a cut or sore in your mouth.

Unless you've never had sex before, you should consider getting an AIDS test prior to engaging in sexual activity, and you should ask your partner to do the same. Other than abstinence, latex condoms are the best protection against the sexual transmission of AIDS and other STDs (though nothing is foolproof), and you're *crazy* if you don't use them, even if you're also using another form of birth control. A secondary benefit of always using condoms is that if you have a "next partner," you can assure them you've never engaged in sex without a condom.

Contraceptives

There are a number of places where you can get condoms. Drugstores sell them. Sometimes university health services and student groups distribute them for free, and campus bathrooms sometimes have condom vending machines.

But arranging for contraceptives—whether it's picking up a condom or heading to the doctor's office to get a prescription for the Pill—can be nerve-wracking for some.

From: Macani
To: Craig
Sent: Monday, March 7, 12:30 PM
Subject: no big deal

Finally went to the doctor to get the Pill. Remember how freaked out I was by the idea of some doctor asking me all these questions about my sex life and jabbing me? Well, it's less of a big deal than I thought. I guess it's boring for them because they do it all day long. It's practically like my old job at Crispy Burger.

"I'll have a Pap smear, the Pill, and a Diet Coke."

"Extra large?"

"On second thought, I'll have the Fun Meal."

"That is the Fun Meal."

Anyway, glad to get that over with. Be happy you're not a girl.

Macani

As Macani suggests, the process isn't so bad. Talking about your sexual history and asking questions about STDs and contraceptives is less embarrassing than you might imagine, simply because these doctors, nurses, and receptionists aren't embarrassed by anything. And their being unflappable cuts the average flappableness in the room by half.

Your job: get educated. If you're a woman, you're probably already aware that you can't get pregnant from kissing a guy. But you can get pregnant the first time you have sex. You can get pregnant from one sexual encounter. You can get pregnant if you don't have an orgasm. And you can get pregnant during your period.

It's crucial that each partner get up-to-date, detailed information about contraception to determine which form is right for you. Types of contraception include barrier methods (condom, diaphragm, and cervical cap); hormonal methods (birth control pills, Norplant, Depo-Provera); intrauterine devices; periodic abstinence ("the rhythm method"); and, in conjunction with certain other forms, spermicides. Each form of contraception has benefits and drawbacks to consider, and you might want to use some combination of them. For example, hormonal contraceptives help prevent pregnancy, but they don't protect against STDs. Prior to engaging in sexual activity, you should talk with a doctor to see which form of contraceptive makes the most sense for you and your partner.

Don't use the "withdrawal method." A word of caution on a form of "contraception" that is really no contraception at all: the withdrawal method. Some couples assume that if the man withdraws prior to ejaculation, conception will be prevented. There are two problems with this thinking, in addition to the fact that it does nothing to protect against STDs. The first is that sometimes men do not end up withdrawing, despite an intention to do so. The second is that women can get pregnant even from pre-ejaculatory fluids. So don't take the risk.

The morning-after pill. If you have engaged in unprotected sex and fear you may be pregnant, consider talking with a health care professional to discuss whether emergency contraception (the so-called morning-after pill) is available and appropriate (you should do this within five days, and ideally, within three). When you talk to your doctor, gather as much information as possible about how the pill works, safety, side effects, and the full range of choices.

Pregnancy

If a woman gets pregnant by accident, it raises a number of difficult issues. You'll have to make choices about whether and how to tell the guy who got you pregnant, and whether and how to tell your parents, family, and friends.

You'll have to decide whether to carry the pregnancy to term or have an abortion. If you choose to carry the pregnancy to term, you'll have to decide whether to keep the child or put it up for adoption, and perhaps whether or not to stay with or marry the father. There exist sharply conflicting views about abortion and adoption, but ultimately, the decision about what to do lies with the woman who is pregnant.

These are big decisions and can involve tremendous anxiety. Feelings of fear, guilt, or shame are not uncommon, and women can sometimes feel isolated and alone. But there's no reason a woman should have to confront these issues without support. Having one or two good friends or family members to talk with about what's going on can be invaluable, and virtually every campus has health care professionals ready to counsel any of the various parties involved. They will not only help educate a woman about her options, but will help her deal with the emotional impact as well.

The men involved can also endure serious stress and emotional turmoil. They find themselves having to look out for their own emotional needs, while at the same time trying to figure out how to help someone else. None of it is easy.

Perhaps the best advice if you're a guy is to make sure you're getting help if you need it. At the same time, you have to remember that you have the responsibility to offer support to the woman involved, if she wants it. That support can be emotional in nature—going with her to find out about the options, going with her to get an abortion, going with her to an adoption agency. Or the support may be financial. You might pay for expenses associated with an abortion, or, far more significantly, you might be expected to pay for the expenses associated with raising a child.

If this all sounds like serious stuff, it is. That's why it's so important to discuss these issues before having sex, and to use contraception.

ALCOHOL AND SEX

We talked about issues relating to alcohol in Chapter 2, but they're worth talking about again. For better or worse, alcohol often plays a part in the sex lives of college students. Too often, it's for worse.

For some people, consuming alcohol has the following effects: it increases their desire to have sex; lowers their inhibitions; makes them more aggressive; reduces their concern about future consequences; and destroys their ability to know what they want and to understand what someone else is communicating.

Under those influences, it's hard to make smart decisions about sex. That's why if you insist on drinking, you should build in some structural safety nets, including these:

1. Don't Drink for the First Time at a Party

Many college students don't drink at all; others have their first drink while in college, most likely during freshman year. The mix of first-time drinkers and big parties is particularly dangerous. If you don't know your reaction to having one drink—

or five—you might find yourself feeling more intoxicated or out of control than you assumed you would, and that can lead to consequences that are devastating, whether sexual or otherwise.

2. Go to Parties with a Friend

Particularly if you're going to a big social event, or a party that is at a fraternity or at another school, go with friends. You should look out for each other, and each take responsibility for making sure the others get home safely. Make agreements in advance about when to come home and how to get there safely.

3. Be Cautious About Going to Someone's Room

This doesn't mean that if you go to a guy's room after having a few drinks, he's going to try to rape you. And it certainly doesn't mean if you go to someone's room and something bad does happen that it was somehow your fault. But still, it's best to be careful. If you've both had a number of drinks, then being by yourself in a room with someone—especially someone you don't know well—can be unwise.

If you *do* decide to go to someone's room, make sure that you tell a friend where you're going, and make sure the person whose room you're going to knows that your friends know where you're going.

4. Look After a Friend Who Has Had Too Much to Drink

If a friend is drunk or out of control and appears on the verge of getting into a sexually dangerous situation, do your best to intercede. That applies whether your friend is male or female. Your friends are responsible for themselves, of course, and they may not listen to you or may even get angry that you're interfering. But you could be saving them from a terrible situation.

RAPE AND SEXUAL ASSAULT

Acquaintance rape and sexual assault are serious problems on college campuses. They can have a devastating impact on survivors, as well as on friends and family and members of the larger community. Students who have been raped often suffer from depression and/or post-traumatic stress. Their course work and extracurricular activities often suffer major disruption, and some rape survivors end up taking time off or even transferring to a different school.

Offenders can be expelled from school or prosecuted under the criminal justice system. Crimes like rape and sexual assault can carry long jail terms. There is a growing awareness that some men who commit rape on campus do so with premeditation. The victim is chosen in advance; alcohol is often involved and, increasingly, so is the use of so-called knock-out or date rape drugs. (Because of this risk, you should only drink when you know what's in your glass, and if you leave your drink unattended, get a new drink.)

Most men, of course, have no intention of raping or hurting anyone, but even so, there are a few bedrock rules that everyone should be aware of. First, the fact that a woman agrees to come back to your room, or invites you to hers, doesn't mean she is consenting to fool around or have sex. Second, it's important to be aware that being drunk or impaired is not a defense against charges of rape or assault. You're *always* responsible for your actions.

At the same time, if the person you want to have sex with is impaired, he or she may not be deemed "competent" to give consent. Consent has to be explicit and clear, and the person who gives it must be competent to do so. If you're wondering how drunk is too drunk, you're already way over the line of reasonable (and possibly legal) behavior.

If You've Been Raped

People who have been sexually assaulted or raped can be traumatized by the experience, and are often left feeling a range of powerful emotions—rage, vulnerability, fear, shame, depression, panic, emptiness.

In the confusion that ensues, many people are uncertain about what to do. They may be in a state of shock, or simply afraid of what will happen. It's common for rape survivors to wonder who they can really trust, whether they'll be judged, and whether, if they seek help, they'll lose control of what happens next.

It's crucial that women and men who have been raped or assaulted recognize that what happened is *never* their fault. Going to talk to someone at health services as soon as possible is one of the best things a person can do. Counselors will be unconditionally supportive, and there's no substitute for talking with someone you trust who really understands what you're going through.

You don't need to have made any decisions before seeking help. Part of the benefit of going to health services is that counselors there can help you work through the confusing mess of emotions, and they can talk to you about what else, if anything, you might do next. But they'll leave the choice for what to do up to you. (In Chapter 9 we talk further about issues around getting help.)

If a Friend Has Been Raped

Your number one role if a friend has been raped is to just "be there." Listen to your friend. Let her know you care. Let her know she can count on you. Don't try to figure out what happened. Don't try to help her figure out "why" it happened. Don't tell her what to do. Just be there, and listen, and care.

You might find out about what resources are available, and when the moment seems right, share what you've learned with your friend. (The Appendix lists a number of valuable resources in addition to your school's health services.) If your friend decides to get help, offer to go with her. If her condition becomes an emergency (as we'll discuss further in Chapter 9), then you should call an administrator, health services, or the police, and ask their advice about what role you can play and what you should do.

As the friend of a rape survivor, there are serious stresses on you as well. Don't forget to look out for your own emotional well-being, and don't hesitate to seek help for yourself if you need it.

8
Parents

From: Rollo
To: Attorney David Ritchie, at Ritchie & Ritchie
Sent: Thursday, November 27, 8:16 PM
Subject: Rollo Sr.

Dear Attorney Ritchie:

I write to request a consultation on how I might become legal guardian of my father. He appears to have contracted one of those Oliver Sacks mistake-your-wife-for-a-hat diseases. In the weeks since my departure for college, he has purchased a dilapidated old boat that he visits at every opportunity. He affectionately refers to this boat as his "very own fixer-upper." That was my name.

Whereof, I remain,
Rollo

By "parents" we mean the person or people who raised you, or the adult you call when you call home. That could be your grandmother, a single parent, or a stepparent. What matters is that you love this person, that they love you, and that more than occasionally, you have fights.

This chapter is about those fights. It's about the big things, like burdensome parental expectations and disagreements over money, and the little things, like phone calls that always seem to come at the wrong time. It's about what causes the tensions between parents and their kids, and how to talk about these problems in ways that actually help.

EXPECTATIONS EXPLAINED

All parents have expectations of their kids. It's just part of being a parent. For some students, parental expectations provide a useful goal to strive toward. For others, parental expectations can feel like a lifelong burden, a backpack full of heavy, jagged rocks with no room to add anything of your own.

Hearing Expectations as Disapproval

Why is it that some students take their parents' expectations in stride, while others stagger under their weight? The answer has to do with what their parents' expectations mean to them. If you hear your parents' expectations as a withholding of love or approval, that's a lot of weight to bear. If, instead, expectations are built on a foundation of love and approval, then they are more easily heard as guidance and goals.

When expectations are heard as disapproval, the conversation becomes strained and confusing. Your parents offer advice; you get angry. Your parents wonder why you're so defensive and stubborn; you wonder why your parents don't offer more love and support.

And being off at college, you might feel particularly vulnerable when it comes to your parents' love and approval. You're away from home, confronting endless challenges and uncertainties. You need support more than ever. It's not surprising then that you're sometimes quick to hear advice as criticism and expectations as disapproval. The stress affects your parents as well. In their zeal to help, they can be more overbearing and critical than they intend.

Witness the telephone conversation between Sweeney and his father. Sweeney's father, a salesman, wants him to work as an intern at a law firm for the summer. But Sweeney has his heart set on returning to his job as a lifeguard at the local day camp.

Dad: Teddy, I spoke with your Uncle Frank. He'd be pleased to have you work as an intern at his law firm this summer.

Sweeney: Yeah, you know, I don't know. I'm not sure what I want to do.

Dad: I think this is a good way to try out the legal field. Worst-case scenario, you don't like it. But maybe you will. I think you would make a fine lawyer.

Sweeney: I was still thinking about that lifeguard job.

Dad: The lifeguard job? Teddy, this will be four summers of that. There's no advantage to doing it for another year.

Sweeney: Dad, they really want me again.

Dad: They can want you all they like, but at some point you have to step up to the plate and get a real job.

Sweeney: Dad, why don't you just let me worry about this, okay?

Dad: Look, son, you happen to be lucky enough to have an uncle who can give you a great job. I just don't want you to make a shortsighted decision you'll come to regret.

Sweeney: Yeah, well, whose decision is it?

Dad: I'll tell you what. You give this some thought. You give it some serious thought.

What does Sweeney make of this conversation? Here's how he puts it to Duncan:

From: Sweeney
To: Duncan
Sent: Wednesday, March 2, 11:10 PM
Subject: Take this job and shove it

Hey man, just got off the phone with my dad to talk about my summer plans. I was hoping the conversation would go like this:

Me: Dad, I'm going to be a lifeguard again this summer.

Dad: Good for you, son. Even I know that college boys need hot girls year-round.

Me: Word.

In fact, the conversation went like this:

Dad: Son, you're a horrible disappointment. I think you're a loser, your mother thinks you're a loser, and let's face it, even

Uncle Frank thinks you're a loser. But at least he's willing to give you a summer job at his law firm.

Me: Well, all the more reason for me to become a career lifeguard.

Dad: No, son. Because if you take a job with Uncle Frank, we can at least maintain the delusion that you'll become a successful lawyer one day.

Man, I wish I had your parents. They're going to let you lifeguard, right?

Sweeney

Where Expectations Come From

Does Sweeney's note to Duncan capture how his father really feels? Probably not. What Sweeney hears as disapproval and disappointment isn't intended that way by his father. What's actually going on for his father is more complicated than Sweeney suspects.

Here are some of the typical concerns that go into parental expectations:

"I don't want you to make the mistakes I've made." Often, parents develop expectations for their children based on their own wrong turns or unmet expectations of themselves.

Sweeney Sr. always wanted to be a lawyer, but at the time he considered going to law school, he made the decision to return home and care for his mother who was ill. Eventually, the law school dream faded, and he became a salesman instead.

Though he's been successful, Sweeney's father continues to regret never having gotten a graduate degree. He knows he's at least as bright as his brother Frank, and feels he would have been stimulated by the intellectual challenge of being a lawyer. He doesn't want his son to have the same regrets that he himself has. (Interestingly, Frank always wished he had gone into sales.)

"I worry about you." Parents worry about their children far more than they let on. After worrying about your current physical health and safety, the next thing on their worry list is your future health and safety. Accordingly, they often favor activities and careers that will keep you as financially secure as possible.

Over the years, when the economy has entered a downturn, the Sweeneys have been hit hard. The family has suffered, and this has been a source of some pain and even shame for Sweeney's dad. He has observed his lawyer brother weathering the downturns more easily. He doesn't want his son to have to endure the same sorts of hardships.

"I want you to be fulfilled." Job One for a parent is to keep you safe. Job Two is to see you fulfilled and happy. Your parents want you to share their values and to pursue what is meaningful to you. But it's not always easy to figure out how to help someone else be fulfilled. So sometimes parents judge based on things that are easy to quantify, like "Are you getting good grades?" and "Are you making good money?" If they could figure out some way to know for sure that you were happy and fulfilled, they'd care a lot less about these other things. But since they can't, they keep harping on [fill in their current obsession].

"I've been around the block." Sweeney Sr.'s advice also comes from an awareness that he knows some things about life that Sweeney doesn't. It's not that he's smarter or knows more facts. It's that he's lived through more stages of life than Sweeney, and has some perspective about the way people can change as they get older.

He doesn't know that his son will change in the same ways, but he assumes he might. In a sense, he sees himself as a messenger from the future, bearing a message about what's important in life and how to make wise choices. It's no wonder then that Sweeney Sr. is frustrated with his son. It's always frustrating when you're trying to deliver a message and no one is listening, especially if that message feels urgent.

How to Have the Conversation

Once you see where some of Sweeney Sr.'s expectations come from, it's easier to keep things in perspective. His reaction is more about fear and concern than any sort of disapproval, and finding ways to discuss those will help the conversation between Sweeney and his parents—or you and your parents—go more smoothly.

Don't use hit-and-run phone messages or e-mails. If there's something you want to tell your parents that might surprise or upset them, don't do it in a brief phone message:

- "Hey, Mom. Decided to drop out. Okay, bye."
- "Hi, folks. How's everything at home? Hope the cat is feeling better. And how are the neighbors? Did you ever agree on who was going to pay to cut down the tree? Nothing

much new here. I got put on academic probation today. Love you."
- "It's me, your daughter. Remember that whole conversation we had about me not getting married to the guy in federal prison? Well, too late."

Admittedly, some things are really hard to say, and maybe you can't imagine telling your parents something disappointing face to face. In that case, writing an e-mail can be useful, if it acts as the *start* of a conversation.

A good e-mail conveys the information ("I really want to lifeguard this summer") and explains the background and reasoning ("Here's why it's so important to me"). It also acknowledges that your parents might see it differently ("I know you feel really strongly that this isn't the best thing for me"), and invites further conversation ("I want to hear more about your concerns. Let's find a time to talk this through").

Ask, "What are you most concerned about?" It may seem crazy, but it's actually helpful *to you* if your parents are able to talk about their underlying concerns. Too often, they translate their actual concerns into advice that may or may not be helpful: "Do this, do that." But what they really mean is, "I'm worried about this. I'm worried about that." Think about it: it's easier to deal with your parents' fears and concerns than with their random demands.

For example, when Sweeney's father said, "At some point you have to step up to the plate," Sweeney responds with, "Why don't you let me worry about this?" Instead, Sweeney might say, "It sounds like you're worried about me getting a good job when I graduate." In response, his father can talk a little about his own life and what he's learned. And he can express his concerns about Sweeney choosing a career that's more secure than his.

Sweeney doesn't have to agree with his father. He can show he understands his father's concerns without saying, "I agree with you that I should work at the law firm." Asking questions and understanding the concerns is different from going along with the suggestion.

Don't say, "It doesn't matter." Admit: "Yeah, I'm worried too." Sweeney assumes that if he lets his father know the truth—that he's also anxious about his future—it will just add fuel to the fire. But it has the opposite effect. Sweeney Sr. wants to know that Sweeney is taking his future seriously, and that he's taking it into account when he makes his decision about the summer. When Sweeney says, "I'm not worried," his father hears it as, "I don't really understand how the world works."

Instead, Sweeney should be clear about what he's really thinking: "I get really anxious about what I'm going to do also. I think about it all the time. If I worked with Uncle Frank, I'd probably learn a lot, and so I know it's a big loss if I don't. But it's really important to me to have this summer with my friends." This at least lets his father know that Sweeney understands the true nature of the decision. And surprisingly, it makes it more likely that Sweeney Sr. will go along with his son's desires.

Raise the bigger issues: "I want you to be proud of me." We said earlier that a big piece of the puzzle has to do with whether you feel loved and accepted by your parents. From your point of view, that concern is more important than any particular choice you make about a summer job. And it's in the not-so-distant background of all the conversations you have with your parents.

Issues of love and acceptance between parent and child can be exceedingly complex, and there's no easy fix. But it's helpful to remember that different people show love in different ways. Some parents have trouble expressing love directly, so they demonstrate caring by paying for school or pestering you about your health or by giving advice.

If you decide to talk with your parents about these issues, be thoughtful about how you raise the subject. Don't say, "You don't care about me!" It's too easy to turn that into an argument. Instead, say something like, "Sometimes I wonder whether you're proud of me," or, "The burden of trying to live up to your expectations has been really hard for me. Sometimes I just want to hear that you're on my side."

It may take a number of conversations over time before they start to get it. But if it's something you feel strongly about, it may be worth taking the emotional risk of talking about how you feel.

Problem-solve: "Let's think about what to do." The tendency in these tough conversations is either to give in against your will or to storm off and do whatever you want. But there may be other solutions to the problem that neither you nor your parents have considered. Sweeney, for example, might agree to get a part-time legal intern job during sophomore year, or take a class in legal history, or spend a couple of weeks before lifeguarding season working at his uncle's firm. The goal is to try to come up with something that works for everyone.

DAY-TO-DAY ANNOYANCES EXPLAINED

Macani and her parents have a great relationship, but still, they have their issues. Macani puts it this way: "My parents' primary hobby in life is to find new and exciting ways to annoy me." Here's a typical interaction.

Dad: Hi, Macani, it's Dad. We tried calling you earlier but you're never there. We talked to your roommate, though. Such a nice girl.

Macani: Hi, Dad. I don't really have time to talk right now, I gotta get this paper done. Can I call you tomorrow?

Dad: [Father talks at length about his day.]

Macani: Dad, you know what, I can't talk right now—

Dad: —Do you want to talk to your mother? [Puts mother on the phone.]

Mom: Hi, honey. Have you bought a ticket home for Christmas yet?

Macani: No. Not yet. Mom, I'm just in the middle of this paper—

Mom: —The trains are getting full, and if you think they care if there's room for you, they don't. I don't understand why you haven't booked a ticket yet.

Macani: You know, I was telling Dad, I'm really busy—

Mom: Well, I don't want to distract you from your hard work. Now your father, there's someone who works hard. He's played so many weddings this month it's a wonder he doesn't keel over with a heart attack. But thank God he has the work, with your tuition as high as it is . . . [More free association from mother.] Okay, Macani, we love you.

What They Mean, What You Hear

Like the Professor Translator, the chart below breaks down what Macani's parents actually say, how Macani hears it, and what her parents actually mean.

PARENTS SAY	MACANI HEARS	PARENTS MEAN
"You're never there."	"We don't trust you. Lord knows what crazy things you're off doing."	"You never seem to have time to talk and are always so anxious. I miss you and wish I knew what was going on in your life."
"You need to buy a ticket home."	"You're undisciplined, slovenly, and lack organizational skills."	"I want to be helpful. Until I know for sure how you're getting home, I'll worry about it."
"Your father is working so hard . . . it's a wonder he doesn't keel over with a heart attack."	"Your father's untimely death will be on your hands. The only way to atone will be to do 'whatever your father would have wanted.' Feeling guilty is a good but meager start."	"Why are you always trying to get off the phone? Maybe you don't appreciate us. I better think of something that gets your attention and reminds you how much we love you."
"Love you."	"We would love you more if you called more, didn't make us so worried all the time, and became a doctor. As it is, we love you medium-well."	"Love you."

We begin to get a sense for the disconnect here, but there's more to the picture. Like Sweeney, Macani is missing some of what's really going on with her parents.

Connection versus Independence

For Macani's parents, these conversations are at heart about connection. Macani may not live at home anymore, but her parents want to feel like they're still part of her life. The more Macani seems distracted or hurried, and the more she asserts her independence, the stronger their desire for connection becomes.

Your going to college can mean big changes for your parents. Though having other siblings at home can help, your parents are still grappling with the fact that the central focus of their lives for the last eighteen years (you) isn't around. They've been dreading (and anticipating) this moment since the day you were born. They don't want you to feel sad or guilty, so they might not go around telling you how much they miss you, but they do.

The problem is that your parents' desire for connection often sounds like them "checking up on you" or "not trusting you." It can also turn into constant advice-giving or nagging. "Have you bought your ticket?" "No." "How about now?" "No." "How about now?" "No!" Eventually, someone will lose their temper and possibly their mind.

From: PJ
To: Macani
Sent: Monday, December 6, 7:55 PM
Subject: message

Hey Macani,

Your parents just called my cell phone, saying that our room phone was disconnected and they wondered whether the dorm burned down. I told them it hadn't. Then they wanted to know if you had burned down, and I told them you haven't to my knowledge.

 I know you're sick of talking to them, but maybe you should plug the phone back in.

PJ

Four Things That Help

When it comes to managing the question of how and how often to talk with your parents, what you *do* is more important than what you *say*. Regardless of how much you tell them you care about them and want to talk to them, they won't buy it if, like Macani, you're always trying to hang up. Here are a few tips on satisfying your parents that won't require you to duct-tape your hand to the phone.

   1. Be the one who calls or e-mails. Don't always wait for your parents to call you. By far the most powerful way to let your parents know that you love and appreciate them is to give them a call occasionally. More than anything you can say, the gesture of being the one to call is hard evidence of your desire to stay connected.

There are side benefits too. If you call your parents periodically, they're less likely to call at just the wrong times. It may never be the absolute perfect time to talk, but if you get to pick the time, odds are, it'll be better than if they pick the time.

2. Give your parents undivided attention. Your parents aren't stupid. They can tell when you're only half listening, or watching TV or reading e-mail while you're talking. The truth is, fifteen minutes of your undivided attention is far better from their point of view than an hour of you fading in and out. So when you're talking with your parents, really be there.

3. Don't promise to call later and then not call. When you say, "Let's talk later," you may mean, "later tonight or later next week or whenever." But your parents hear "later tonight." They might be looking forward to talking with you, and may worry if they don't hear from you. They might even change their plans. If you can't talk now, say so. But don't raise their expectations and then let them down.

4. Give them reassurance. If you keep feeling nagged or like your parents are always suspicious about what you're doing, it may be that you just aren't giving them enough information for them to feel reassured about your well-being.

They can't help it. Their parental instincts kick in. They need reassurance. The less you tell them, the more it seems like you're hiding something, and the more worried they feel. So be forthcoming when you can. Don't just call when you're homesick or need advice. Call with good news as well, even if the news seems small. It will mean more to them than you might imagine.

TALKING ABOUT MONEY

From: Rollo
To: Mom & Dad
Sent: Tuesday, February 8, 10:22 PM
Subject: gainful employment

Dear Parents,

I have been wracked with guilt of late, knowing that the tuition bill you paid last month would have served equally well to renovate your kitchen or to buy a Cadillac.

Forthwith, I have acquired gainful employment sufficient to cover my daily expenses and books. My new job with the State Consumer Protection Office provides the added benefit of free legal counsel in the event that I am sued by a large corporation.

Much Love,
Rollo

P.S. Please disregard the cease and desist letter you received from Krispy Kreme. My peeps at the CPO have got it covered.

Despite the availability of financial aid and loans, paying for college is a strain on almost all families. The strain can highlight and deepen already existing tensions between parent and student.

As you talk to your parents about money, remember that it's never *only* about money. There's always something else going on, and getting a handle on that something else is the first step in dealing with these issues.

Guilt

The more you observe your parents sacrificing, the more potential there is for you to feel guilty about it. The best way to manage feelings of guilt is to figure out what the guilt "means." It may mean that you appreciate your parents more than ever. If so, tell them how much their sacrifices mean to you. You may assume they already know, and maybe they do. But tell them anyway.

Feelings of guilt might also arise from your sense that you aren't putting enough effort into college to justify the expense and sacrifice. If that's the case, it may be that feeling guilty is a sign that you should study harder and party less. Or it may be an opportunity to take stock of what you want to get out of your college years.

Control

What is your parents' role in the choices you make? Should you major in engineering because your parents want you to, even though you want to study the classics? And what impact, if any, does their financial support have on what you decide? The relationship between money and control is a thorny one.

Some parents try to stay out of all this. They figure that one of the most important lessons their child will learn at school is how to make decisions and live with the consequences. Other parents expect to have more input. Especially if it's a big decision, they want some say, and maybe even the final say.

What role *should* a parent have in a college student's decisions? This question implicates issues of culture, personal values, and parenting style. But here's what we know: students who are unhappy with what they are majoring in, or who feel like they had no choice in the matter, tend to do worse than students who like what they're majoring in and feel ownership over the choice.

Why? Because if you're good at something, you tend to like it, and if you like something, you tend to spend more time on it. A student who has ownership over the choice is more likely to feel invested in making the decision work. Students who make their own decisions are also more likely to develop a sense of responsibility for their lives—an awareness that what they do and how hard they try contributes to their success or failure. And students who make their own decisions are getting practice making decisions, which is a crucial life skill.

That said, there's an important role for parental input, whether or not parents are contributing financially. If parents see their job as enforcing their own will or overruling their child's preferences, it can lead to trouble. But parents can play a crucial role in helping students think more clearly about their choices. They can help them think realistically about the potential consequences of a particular choice and what it would mean to accept responsibility for those consequences.

How should you respond if your parents link financial support to selecting a particular major? Your overwhelming urge will be either to give in, which can lead to resentment, or to call your parents' bluff: "Great, I'll drop out of school and get a job flipping burgers if that makes you happy!"

You can't control whether your parents choose to contribute to your schooling. What you can do is try to keep the conversation on a positive track. When they say, "We won't pay," instead of arguing, you should empathize: "I didn't realize how important this was to you. You must be really concerned." You also have to try to explain how you feel—what engineering means to you, what the classics mean to you, and how you see the choice of a major playing out in your life.

It can be terrifying when parents threaten to withdraw financial support. It can be equally painful for parents to watch a child make what they consider to be a major life mistake. But sometimes the hardest conversations are also the most important.

Responsibility

Do your parents often bail you out of messes, whether academic, financial, or otherwise? If so, you're asking for their help in exchange for freedom you might otherwise enjoy.

The best way to ease them out of the job as your personal caretakers is for you to be responsible—aggressively responsible—for running your own life. Here's what that *doesn't* look like:

- "I bought my girlfriend this amazing necklace, and it really meant a lot to her. Now my parents are saying I'm supposed to pay the credit card bill myself. How am I supposed to come up with that kind of cash?"

- "I rented this video and when I returned it, it was a little overdue, maybe a couple of months or something. And my parents are all mad over the late fine. Hey, I didn't even like the movie, and anyway, my parents were the ones who forgot to remind me it was due."

- "I want to go to Florida over spring break, but my parents won't pay for it. They say I have to get a job on campus if I want to go. Screw that! How am I supposed to learn how to be independent if they won't even let me go on a trip?"

You get the idea. Part of how your parents treat you is based on *your own behavior*. If you want your parents to trust you, you have to be trustworthy. If you want them to turn control of your life over to you, you have to demonstrate responsibility. It's not enough to be *usually* trustworthy or responsible. You can't say, "Well, I borrowed the car five times and I only crashed it once. So mostly, I'm a good driver." It doesn't work that way. The standard is "always," not "usually."

The good news is this: once you start demonstrating that you're on top of things—that your financial situation is under control, that you know deadlines for things, that you can manage your own life—you'll notice that your parents treat you differently. As you demonstrate more responsibility, you'll get more freedom.

Identity

For better or worse, money and self-image can be closely tied. Depending on how your family has traditionally treated money, letting your parents know you're having money troubles can be a painful conversation—not just because the topic itself is complex, but because you feel like you're letting yourself and others down.

It's important to remember that parents can have these issues as well. Some parents feel tremendous pride at having gotten you through year eighteen, and they figure college is pretty much up to you. Others wish they could contribute more to your education, and feel a sense of shame at not being able to.

So when you're talking with your parents about money, remember that just as it can be a sensitive issue for you, it can be a sensitive issue for them as well. If emotions come up during the conversation that you didn't expect, it may be because there are some identity issues in the background.

A Note on Spending

There's really only one rule about spending money during college: *don't spend money you don't have.*

Most students are responsible with money and follow this rule. But some feel like they are entitled to a certain lifestyle, whether they have the money to pay for it or not—and that's trouble. If you live at school and are on the meal plan, then virtually any additional expenses (except for books and other course-related purchases) are optional. It may not feel that way. You may think, "Well, my friends eat out twice a week, so obviously I'm going to go with them" or, "I can't live without cable." All of which is fine if you can pay for it.

But if you can't, you can't. Living within your means is about recognizing that you can't have certain things, even things you desperately want or think you deserve. It may be reasonable to hope your parents contribute to your tuition, but it's not reasonable to think they're supposed to pay for you to have cable or a cell phone or a car or a stereo system or dinners out.

Credit. If you want to buy nonessentials on credit, think it through in advance. Consider how much money you'll have coming in and what you'll be required to pay out. If you can make it work, then it's okay to use credit. If not, don't. Failing to keep up with a credit card means you'll be paying out huge monthly payments just to cover the interest and to avoid penalties. Getting out from under that burden is the last thing you need to take on in college.

If you don't trust yourself with a credit card, consider getting a debit card from your bank instead. This is a card that lets you charge up to the amount you have in your bank account, but offers more convenience than writing an actual check.

A Note on Working

Whether you come from a family where money is tight or a family that has already donated a building in your name, getting a part-time job in college is a great thing to do. Research has found that having a part-time job doesn't affect grades. The extra money can be used to pay some tuition or, if it's not needed for that, to buy the things you want.

Even more important than the money is the sense you get of contributing to your own education. People who help pay for their education are less likely to take it for granted and feel more freedom to make choices that suit them. And nothing teaches you that you can make it in the "real world" better than actually making it in the real world.

9
Mental Health

From: Rollo
To: Director, Centers for Disease Control
Sent: Tuesday, September 7, 6:56 PM
Subject: a little bit anxious

Dear Mr. or Ms. Director,

I recently attended the mandatory mental health outreach session our RA held for our dorm. At this session, we learned about anorexia, bulimia, overeating, alcohol abuse, depression, anxiety, insomnia, drug abuse, homesickness, social isolation, parental pressure, low self-esteem, and pinkeye.

I was disappointed that hypochondria was not covered because I am worried I might be suffering from it. I would appreciate it if you could fill me in on its symptoms, so I can make an informed self-diagnosis.

On an unrelated note, I wonder whether you might consider placing my roommate under quarantine. I'm not sure what he

> has, but I don't think he should be walking about giving it to the rest of us.
>
> Rollo

As Rollo's e-mail points out, college students grapple with a number of mental health and well-being issues. These issues are surprisingly common—in the real world and on campus. (The prevalence of mental health problems among college students is about the same as in the general population.) There's still a stigma surrounding mental illness. Too often, students who are suffering try to hide it from their friends, and end up suffering alone.

Whether you're battling your own demons or trying to figure out how best to help a friend, *everyone* comes in contact with some sort of mental health issue by the time they graduate. This chapter offers an overview of some of the more common problems that students face—depression, eating issues, anxiety, addiction, and trauma. We also discuss typical concerns students have about seeking help, and in the last section of the chapter, we offer some thoughts on how to talk to someone you're worried about.

DEPRESSION

Depression is one of the most common mental health problems, affecting about one in ten college students. Of course, everyone feels down on occasion. No one gets through life without encountering periods of loss, longing, and loneliness.

But sadness and depression are two different things. Sadness is a heightened emotional state, and in that sense, even though sadness is painful, it's very much about being alive and in the world. We can learn when we're sad, connect with others, and connect with ourselves. Our lives still have meaning.

SYMPTOMS OF DEPRESSION

Not everyone who is depressed experiences every symptom. Some people experience a few symptoms, some many. Symptoms include:

- Persistent sad, anxious, or "empty" mood
- Feelings of hopelessness, pessimism
- Feelings of guilt, worthlessness, helplessness
- Loss of interest or pleasure in hobbies and activities that were once enjoyed, including sex
- Decreased energy, fatigue, being "slowed down"
- Difficulty concentrating, remembering, making decisions
- Insomnia, early-morning awakening, or oversleeping
- Appetite and/or weight loss or overeating and weight gain
- Thoughts of death or suicide; suicide attempts
- Restlessness, irritability
- Persistent physical symptoms that do not respond to treatment, such as headaches, digestive disorders, and chronic pain

From the National Institute of Mental Health—http:// www.nimh.nih.gov

---

People who are depressed tend to feel disconnected from the world. They might feel exhausted, overwhelmed, empty, or weighed down by a crushing despair. Things they used to like no longer give them joy; things that motivated them might now feel pointless. Depression is often accompanied by dread and hopelessness—the sense that how you feel today is how you will feel forever.

Some depressions descend on people with no apparent trigger. More often, they arise at least partly as a result of an external event, like getting cut from a team or getting a disappointing grade or from enduring something more serious, such as the death of a parent, rape, or serious injury.

"Why Not Just Be Happy?"

From the outside, it all seems so easy. People who are depressed are often the targets of pep talks about their attitude or habits:

> "Get out of bed and seize the day!"
> "Why be negative? You have everything anyone could want."
> "It's all in your head. Come on out for dinner and you'll be fine."

It is true that sometimes a depression lifts when you simply get out and do things—working out, being with people, studying, joining a club, going on vacation. But sometimes it doesn't. Either way, depression is not "all in your head." It's more useful to think of it as a physical illness or injury. If someone had a broken leg, you wouldn't tell them to just "walk it off," and you wouldn't be surprised if it took them some time before they returned to their jogging regimen. You also wouldn't wonder why someone who "had it all" was complaining about having the stomach flu. The stomach flu can afflict anyone, and so can depression.

From: PJ
To: Macani
Sent: Thursday, February 3, 6:56 PM
Subject: Cold

Hey Macani,

Hope I didn't wake you when I left this morning at 6:15 a.m. I was too restless to stay in bed, so I got up and walked into town. I know, it's too early, too cold, and too far, but I just needed to get away. Walking around that early is like being in a different town, all frozen and silent, like that Robert Frost poem you showed me.

You know how you've been asking me lately if I'm doing okay? Well, since the season ended, I guess I have been feeling kind of bad. The days seem too long and empty, and I end up getting these waves of dread that come from nowhere. When I'm feeling okay, I can't even understand why I ever get this way, but when I get this way, I can't understand why I ever feel happy.

How is it you seem happy all the time? I don't know. None of this probably makes any sense to you anyway. It doesn't even make sense to me. Do you think you'll be back from rehearsal in time to go to dinner? Not in the mood to have dinner alone . . .

PJ

Too often, the chorus of people saying, "Why don't you just get over it?" includes the person who is depressed. Not only do they feel terrible, but they feel guilty or ashamed for feeling terrible, which compounds the problem. But depression is no more your fault than any other illness.

Through a Glass Darkly

When you're depressed, the way you tell the story of your life changes. The past can seem like a long string of failures and regrets, with successes seeming small or accidental. And every version of the future you can imagine seems to promise more of the same.

At times like these, it's crucial to remember that your thoughts are being filtered through how you feel—it's sort of like looking at everything through darkly tinted glasses. When we feel bad in the present, we project that feeling into the future. While it might feel like "truth" to you, it's a distorted way of making sense of things. Often, you only realize just how distorted your thoughts were when the clouds finally lift.

Suicidal Thoughts

A surprising number of college students report having suicidal thoughts. These can range from the simple awareness that suicide is a possibility, to an active longing for death.

Why would a college student, who seemingly has so much to live for, ever think that death is preferable to life? It's almost always a response to deep emotional pain, brought on by depression, bipolar disorder (also called manic depression), schizophrenia (often characterized by a break from reality), or the sense that it's the "only way out" of a bind that has become all-important in a person's thinking.

All you really need to know about suicidal thoughts is that if you or someone you know has them, you need to talk to an administrator, counselor, or health professional immediately. Health services keeps extra appointments open for urgent problems, so you should be able to talk to someone right away, at any time of day or night.

If you suspect that a friend might be considering suicide, it's okay to ask them about it in explicit terms. You won't be putting ideas into their head. You can ask questions like, "Are you thinking about hurting yourself?" or, "Have you been having suicidal thoughts?" If the answer is any version of "yes" or "I guess so," you need to do everything possible to get that person help.

Offer to walk with them down to health services. If they won't go with you, call health services or the police and describe the conversation, and ask them what you should do. If the person seems like they're in really bad shape, stay with them until help arrives. You don't need to do or say anything special; all you need to do is be with them, listen, and let them know you care.

EATING AND BODY IMAGE

Be prepared for your weight to shift when you first get to college. Some people gain weight from the new food choices or from being less active, while others lose weight due to stress or just eating less. Most students find that their weight levels off over time. Even so, many women and a growing number of men struggle during their college years with issues around food and body image.

Negative Body Image

Almost everyone has something they would change about how they look—their hair, their weight, their nose, their physique, their height, their skin—and many people worry about how others "see" them. These concerns are often mixed in with issues of self-esteem and self-worth, and can run quite deep. Going off to college, where you're in a new context and meeting new people, can bring a fresh wave of concerns.

How you *feel* about your body is obviously subjective. But even how you *see* your body can be subjective—distorted by mood, low self-esteem, or illnesses like anorexia.

The familiar advice about body image is to work on things you have control over, like eating healthy, getting exercise, and learning to love yourself the way you are even as you're working toward something different. This is helpful advice to the extent you can follow it, but there are lots of things that make that hard: media images of the "ideal" body; busy schedules; voices from the past telling you that you weren't attractive or good enough; rejection; all the stuff of real life.

The tragedy is that the more time you spend trying to be someone else, the less time you have to do what you enjoy and to invest in what you care about. If body image anxieties are leading to eating issues or physical ailments, or are getting in the way of full engagement in your own life, you should get help.

Eating Disorders

Whether you are struggling with anorexia, bulimia, or other issues around food, eating disorders are *serious* health problems. What might start as a "simple matter of choice or control" can come to feel overpowering and compulsive. Once you go down that road, the disorder can wreak havoc on your body as well as your mind, causing anemia, infertility, liver damage, and osteoporosis. According to the National Institute of Mental Health, young women suffering from anorexia have an annual death rate twelve times higher than their peers.°

There are the classic signs of eating disorders, like the anorexic person who is conspicuously thin and denies that she is restricting her food intake, or the person with bulimia who sneaks off to the bathroom to purge after every meal.

These may be signs of the most serious problems, but they are not the only signs. Even if you are not anorexic or bulimic per se, your routines around food might give you trouble. Are you constantly thinking about when you're going to eat next, how many calories you're going to take in, and how you're going to burn off the calories you consume? Are trips to the dining hall creating more and more stress, and straining your relationships with friends?

How do you feel when your eating or workout patterns are disrupted? How do you react if someone offers you birthday cake at a party or bad weather prevents you from exercising? If things like this seem disproportionately frustrating and upsetting to you, it could be a sign that food is playing a bigger role in your life than it should.

°"The mortality rate among people with anorexia has been estimated at 0.56 percent per year, or approximately 5.6 percent per decade, which is about 12 times higher than the annual death rate due to all causes of death among females ages 15–24 in the general population." National Institute of Mental Health Web site, citing P. F. Sullivan, "Mortality in anorexia nervosa," *American Journal of Psychiatry* 152(7)(1995): 1073–74.

"Why Won't You Just Eat?"

From: Macani
To: PJ
Sent: Friday, March 4, 7:34 PM
Subject: eat!

Hey PJ,

I'm worried about Lucinda. Did you notice how she only ate half a salad at dinner saying that it was gross (which it was, but still)? And then at lunch yesterday she only had a diet soda and said she already ate. Which, she couldn't have, because we walked together to the dining hall from theater class. This has been going on for a while now.

It's almost too stressful for me to eat with her anymore because I just want to say, "Hey, eat a stupid cheeseburger!"

Macani

From the outside, eating disorders can be hard to understand. If, like Macani, you watch a friend eating salad after day, you might wonder why they don't just eat more. There are a lot of theories about what causes eating disorders: a desire for control over your body, when so many other things in your life feel out of control; making unrealistic weight comparisons with other people; a reaction to an unhappy adolescence or difficult family life; a way of dealing with depression or stress; genetic predispositions.

One thing seems clear: even as people coping with disordered eating know that it creates problems in their life, the restrictive eating (or the cycle of binging and purging) *feels* like a solution. It might seem strange to put "not eating" in the category of self-medication, but it probably belongs there. It can grab hold of you, and whatever the initial "cause," it can take on a self-reinforcing life of its own.

Restricted eating, like alcohol or drugs, can increase serotonin levels, brain chemicals related to happiness and feeling high. While you may feel in control by restricting your food intake, it's a little like being behind the steering wheel of a speeding car that has lost its brakes. You're steering the car, and to that degree, you're "in control," but the broader situation is utterly out of control.

This is why telling the person to "eat a stupid cheeseburger" doesn't help. You're telling them eating is good for them, but they hear you saying, "Let go of the steering wheel," and that's terrifying. They know that restrictive eating makes them feel *good*, and who's right about how they feel? All of which means that having a helping conversation with someone with an eating disorder can be enormously frustrating. (We'll talk in greater depth about how to actually have this conversation later in the chapter.)

ANXIETY

From: Macani
To: Craig
Sent: Tuesday, April 26, 3:17 AM
Subject: Hoppetty Hop

Hey Craig,

Lit final tomorrow. Tried to sleep, but felt too anxious. Worried if I fell asleep there would be a 99% chance that I would miss the exam. Got up, did girl push-ups, studied, panicked, studied, played my Sneeze Dog CD loud and sang along, studied, got up and stomped around, studied, played more Sneeze Dog, called/woke up my parents, studied, got a call from my parents to ask if I'm okay and I told them, "Stop bothering me, don't you know I have a final tomorrow?" Googled Sneeze Dog but got only dog training schools because no one at Sneeze Dog has the organizational skills to put up a damn Web page—which, if I worked for Sneeze Dog, would be the very first thing I'd do for them. Sketched out a few ideas for Sneeze Dog home page. . . . Starting to wonder whether it's even worth trying to sleep or should I just stay up and keep studying and take the test then crash . . . Me so sleepy . . .

Macani

Stress has its benefits. Let's say you and a friend are mountain climbing and your friend breaks his leg. The wild adrenaline surge and blinding terror give you the strength to carry your friend hundreds of miles to safety.

Now imagine that instead of mountain climbing, you're simply studying for an exam. Your brain makes a simple request of your body: "I have to study for an exam. Could I have a little adrenaline to get me motivated?" So far, so good. The problem arises if your body misunderstands the request and instead hears: "Friend with broken leg! Need wild adrenaline surge!" What happens? You have enough hormones rushing through your veins to win the World's Strongest Horse Competition, and all you needed to do was a bit of studying.

An occasional sleepless night is not going to do you much harm, nor is some level of discomfort before an exam or having a healthy concern over your parents' reaction to the news that you are thinking of switching majors. Some level of anxiety is normal and, as a motivator, even useful.

But if the dam breaks, the flood of anxiety can be incapacitating. Some people experience anxiety related to performance—taking a test, trying out for a team. Others suffer from what is called social anxiety, which can make a simple visit to the dining hall or engaging in small talk at a party seem excruciating. Still others find themselves worrying about things they have little control over. The ceiling of your room might collapse, and it feels as if thinking about anything else will increase the likelihood that it will actually happen. So you stay vigilant.

In these cases, anxiety has gone from motivator to major problem. Incapacitating anxiety can be brought on by life circumstances, and there is growing evidence that it has a genetic component as well. You may or may not be able to eliminate from your life those things that are causing the anxiety. But if it persists over time, and if the problem feels like it's slipping out of control, it's important to get help.

ADDICTIVE BEHAVIORS

You can get addicted to almost anything. Whether it's alcohol, drugs, gambling, smoking, shopping, eating, flirting, exercising, or playing video games, some people find themselves needing that "hit" to get through the day.

From: Sweeney
To: Rollo
Sent: Thursday, February 24, 2:15 AM
Subject: Cheat code

Rollo—Help. Locked in dead heat with Cube in Barbie Road Rage. Going on day 3. Can't let Cube win. Please send cheat code or shortcut directions—I keep losing time dropping Skipper off at the tanning salon.

   Please help. Must start paper due tomorrow. Or is tomorrow Saturday?

Sweeney

Of course, some addictions are more serious and harder to break than others. Drugs, alcohol, or smoking are physically harmful and can have serious withdrawal symptoms. Other "addictions"—like playing video games or shopping—might better be called compulsive behaviors. But, as with anorexia and bulimia, they too can be forms of self-medication, ways to manage stress or ward off depression or boredom.

Some of these activities, in moderation, are actually therapeutic; playing a half hour of computer games, going to the mall, or taking a long run can be good ways to relax. But when the behavior starts to get in the way of things that really matter—when you find yourself daydreaming about it incessantly and caring less and less about the rest of your life—that's a sign that something is out of balance.

One key to beating an addiction or compulsive behavior is to recognize the cycle that draws you in. You feel down or stressed so you self-medicate with a video game or a drink. And then you feel better. But—and this is the important part—when the "hit" wears off, you feel bad again, often *worse* than you felt before you engaged in the behavior. So you need another hit to alleviate the depression and anxiety you feel after coming down from the prior hit. What feels like the solution is actually making the problem worse.

Breaking an addiction involves enduring a cycle of pain without resorting to the relief the addictive behavior brings. Depending on how compelling and powerful the addiction, this can be extremely difficult. But slowly, whether it's an hour or a week, the pain begins to lift and the compulsion weakens, though the underlying issues and life circumstances that led to the behavior may still remain.

While some people can beat addiction on their own, everyone can benefit from a support system to keep them on the right track. Whether it be an individual counselor, an official support group, or simply family and friends, you need people who are on your side, understand what you're going through, and can help you address the deeper issues that create the addiction in the first place.

TRAUMA AND LOSS

College is part of the real world, and trauma and loss can happen to anyone. A family member dies. A friend is raped. Your parents get divorced.

Feelings associated with great change or loss can be overwhelming. Life is divided into before and after, and you may wonder whether you can ever feel "normal" again. You experience grief and denial, anger and guilt, numbness and pain. Did this *really* happen? Why? How could it? You may feel rage toward God, or yourself, or your family and friends. Or you might feel hardly anything at all, astonished by the inappropriateness of your own indifference. Your friends and roommates may not understand what you're going through, but like you, they're probably doing their best to cope.

As with depression, someone who has endured trauma will often be told that "it's time to get over it," but trauma, like anxiety and depression, can have a large physiological component. Though not all those who experience traumatic events develop post-traumatic stress disorder (PTSD), trauma can affect people above and beyond the familiar feelings of anger, sadness, and loss. Those suffering from PTSD can experience sleep difficulties, nightmares or flashbacks, or heightened levels of anxiety, or can feel detached from everyday life and the people around them.

There is no one-size-fits-all timetable for healing, and trying to impose one on yourself or someone else only creates more stress. Indeed, it may be that you don't "get over" the death of a parent or loss of a friend. Instead, you might find that healing means learning to live with the loss and, in time, to move forward even so.

A word to friends: you might find yourself unintentionally judging someone who is in pain. "They aren't appropriately upset," you think, or perhaps, "They're just wallowing in self-pity." But remember, you don't know what's really going on inside the person. Everyone experiences trauma and loss in their own way, and everyone copes differently.

SHOULD I GET HELP?

There's no clear answer to when you should seek help. If you're thinking about the possibility, or if any of the symptoms or circumstances we describe above strike a chord, getting help might make sense. On the other hand, many students seek help not out of a specific sense of what's wrong but because things don't seem quite right. And that makes sense too.

It's always harder to see problems in ourselves than in others. Ask yourself this: If someone you cared about were struggling with the issues you're struggling with, what would you recommend they do? If you cared about them, if you loved them, you might encourage them to get help. They would have all kinds of reasons for why getting help doesn't make sense, but you would know that they should at least try.

From: Macani
To: Craig
Sent: Thursday, February 10, 5:35 PM
Subject: grrr . . .

Hi Craig,

So PJ wanted me to go with her to the counseling center because she wanted to talk to someone about the whole depression thing. So she goes in to see this lady, and I was sitting in the waiting room, kind of hoping I wouldn't see anyone I knew.

I was rehearsing my line, "Oh, I'm just here waiting for a friend," when Katelyn of all people walks in and is like "Hey, who are you seeing? I've been seeing Ariel, who is totally great." Coming from her, it sounded so cool. (But knowing me, if Katelyn farted, I would go on an all-bean diet.) Anyway, before I knew it I was making all this stuff up about how I was seeing "Charles" and how he had changed my life.

Thankfully, PJ came back before I had to answer any specifics. She seemed pretty satisfied with the lady she talked to, and is actually looking forward to going back. Maybe I should go see Ariel to deal with this lying in front of cool people problem. . . .

Macani

Concerns About Seeking Help

Of course, even if you recognize that you've got a problem, there are a number of reasons you might be reluctant to seek help.

"I'm not that kind of person." Some students worry that people who ask for help are weak or crazy. They just never thought of themselves as the kind of person who needed help, and certainly not the kind of person who needed help with mental health. But more and more, people are realizing that mental health issues are just like any other health problem, and the best thing to do when you have a health problem is to try to get better. The range of people who seek help is huge—athletes, student leaders, professors, people who get A's, people who get D's. People who ask for help do have two qualities in common: they're self-aware enough to know they've got a problem, and they have courage. Asking for help requires both.

"I don't want anyone to find out." Fact is, there are a ton of people you know who have or will seek help, and you have no idea who they are. The only way you could find out is if they told you. Colleges typically keep their counseling and mental health records as confidential as medical records. But if it's something you're worried about, you should ask a counselor about the confidentiality policy.

"I don't want to be a problem for anyone." No one wants to be a burden for others, or create unnecessary problems. Some people worry that getting help will mean diverting resources from the people who "really" need them. But remember, these services are there for *you,* the same way your professors are there for you. You're paying for them whether or not you use them. They aren't just for emergency situations, and asking for help sooner rather than later usually means fewer resources are required to deal with the issues.

The bottom line is that you matter and your mental health matters. If you aren't sure whether getting help makes sense, go in for a consultation, and then decide what to do. The worst that will happen is you'll waste an hour. The upside is that it could improve your college experience, help you thrive in school, or even save your life.

Finding the Right Help

How do you actually go about getting help, and what will you find when you get there? Below, we look at where to go, discuss the nature of counseling, and share a few words about medications.

Where to go. The counseling and psychiatric services that are available to students vary from college to college, so the first step in seeking help is talking to an advisor, or looking online or in campus materials to find out what services are available. In addition, peer counseling hotlines often have great information about student services and how to make use of them.

If you're not sure what resources exist, you can always call the university's health services, and they'll put you in touch with the right people. In an emergency, call the campus police, and they'll also know what to do.

You might also consider other sources of help, including talking with a coach or a professor you've come to know or with a minister or rabbi. These people may be able to help you on their own, or they may suggest that you work with a mental health professional.

Remember, you're in charge—you can change your mind about who to see, you can decide what kind of help you want, and you can even decide in the middle of seeing someone that you don't want assistance anymore. (Your choices are only restricted in the rare case when you pose a threat to yourself or others; in that case, health care providers have an obligation to protect you.)

What is counseling? Counselors and therapists draw on a variety of approaches for helping. Mostly, it involves you describing what's going on in your life, and the counselor listening with an empathetic ear. They'll try to help you sort through what you're feeling and why, and will give you ideas for what might help.

The foundation of helpful assistance is a trusting relationship in which you feel comfortable talking and truly understood. Some counseling is based on helping you gain insights—about life, yourself, and the ways you think, feel, and behave. A counselor might make connections you hadn't seen, or challenge you to see something from a new perspective.

Other counseling is oriented toward the practical. You'll get concrete advice about how to talk to your parents about your grades or sexuality, or assistance in staying motivated to stick to your new diet or study plan.

The nature of the assistance you get depends on the nature and severity of your problem. Some students benefit from seeing a counselor once; other students see someone a few times a year, just to "check in" on things. Still others might want or need sessions on a weekly or even daily basis. Traditionally, sessions are one-on-one, but many students benefit from being in support groups, or programs that are tailored to a particular concern.

Counselors aren't trying to get you to admit things you don't choose to admit, or trick you into talking about things you don't want to discuss. Whether it's about the past or the present, the only things you'll discuss are things you feel comfortable discussing.

None of this is magic, of course, and counseling is rarely a quick fix. It's more akin to having physical therapy after an injury and building muscle strength and range of motion over time. The only difference is that you're developing your emotional muscles rather than physical ones.

Medication. There are now medications that can help treat virtually all of the problems we've discussed in this chapter. There are effective treatments for depression, panic disorder and social anxiety, bipolar disorder, obsessive-compulsive disorder, and various forms of psychosis. Some of the medications that help for these problems are also being used to treat anorexia and bulimia, symptoms of trauma, and various addictions.

Some students worry that doctors will pressure them to take a medication they aren't comfortable with, and wonder whether the medication will somehow change who they are. These are common concerns, but remember, unless you're a danger to yourself or others, you make your own choices about treatment. You should have a thorough discussion with your doctor about side effects and get all your questions answered before you try any medication. Medications are often prescribed in small doses at first, to make sure the patient is comfortable with the effects.

Another reason students don't take medications that might help is that they don't know about them, or don't believe they'll make a difference. Many students have heard of antidepressants like Prozac or Zoloft, but they may not be aware that these and other medications can help even in cases of mild or moderate depression, and can work in the treatment of anxiety as well. The more you know about your options, the more likely you are to find a treatment that helps.

If you do choose to try medication, remember that it isn't always a quick fix either (for example, an antidepressant might take a number of weeks to take effect), and that often medications work best in conjunction with some form of counseling.

TALKING TO A FRIEND YOU'RE WORRIED ABOUT

What can you do for a friend you think needs help? Perhaps you've tried to persuade them to go see someone, and they've resisted. You feel worried, frustrated, and even a little scared. You're at your wit's end and wonder why the conversations so often seem pointless.

One reason trying to help can be so tough is that you and your friend are experiencing the conversation differently. It's almost as if you were in two different worlds. You might give the conversation the label, "I'm trying to help my friend." Your role feels important and virtuous, a sign that you care.

Your friend might label it differently: "My annoying friend is butting in again," or, "My friend always judges me and tries to control my life. Who does he think he is?" To your friend, the mere suggestion of a problem can be enormously threatening. You think you're helping; your friend thinks you're attacking. You both act reasonably given these assumptions.

What to do? These conversations will probably be hard no matter what, but following a few guidelines can make a big difference.

Problems Are More Complicated from the Inside

Other people's problems always seem easier to deal with than your own. You add up what you've observed and heard from your friend, and it fits into a clear pattern with an easy solution. When you see that your roommate isn't going to class, you think, "Well, just go to class and you'll be okay."

But to your roommate it's not so simple. They might be struggling with overwhelming feelings of hopelessness, anxiety, or shame. They know the pressure they're under from their parents to succeed, and feel their whole future hinges on how this one class turns out. Of course, going to class is a good idea. It's just that they're dealing with far more than meets the eye.

Understanding Comes Before Advising

No one takes advice until they feel understood. Why should they? If you don't really know what I'm going through, your advice could be way off base. The whole time you're giving the advice, I'm thinking, "Blah blah blah, you don't understand what I'm going through, so what good is this?" If you don't seek first to understand, you run the risk of being like the proverbial monkey who dove into the water, grabbed a fish, and carried it up a tree in order to save it from drowning.

Don't think of your goal as getting them to get help, or forcing them to admit they have a problem, or having them see that they aren't happy. Those goals will result in a "you against them" dynamic, no matter how carefully you choose your words.

Goals that are more likely to help include listening to your friend or roommate, trying to understand them, showing them you really care about them, and doing whatever you can to be helpful and supportive. So instead of trying to strong-arm the person into admitting they have a problem and seeking help, ask them how things are going: "It seems like you've been really stressed out lately. What's been going on?" "When you think of getting help, what do you worry about?" Don't jump in with answers or reasons why they're right or wrong. Give them some space to think about what's going on and to talk. Once you really understand where their concerns come from, then you can have a meaningful conversation.

None of this means you shouldn't express your opinion. After all, it may be their problem, but it's impacting you, and that part of it can be useful to talk about. So you might say something like, "Sometimes when we get back from dinner, I feel really worried about you. I don't see you eating anything other than vegetables, and I don't know what that means, but it's upsetting to me." Or, "It seems like you've been feeling kind of down lately. I always want to help, but I'm not sure how." Or, "It's painful for me to watch you going through this. It reminds me of times I've struggled with this myself."

It's Not About Magic Words

Sometimes friends and roommates think to themselves, "Well, I would raise this issue with my roommate but I don't want to upset them, and I never know what to say. I'll wait until I can figure out what to say."

But in a sense, the particular words matter less than your intention in saying them. Trust your own instincts and put things into your own words. It's okay to fumble around, to get nervous, to start in one direction and then go in another.

What if your roommate gets defensive or angry? You might say something like this: "I know this is really stressful to talk about. I'm trying to figure out a way to be helpful. It's really hard." If your roommate says, "Well, a way to be helpful would be to stay out of this," you can say, "It's your decision about whether to get help. I just wanted you to know I'm worried about you, and if you want to talk about it, I'm around."

Remember, all you can do is your best. You can let your friend know you care, you can alert an RA or other friends or a college administrator. But in the end, it's their choice about whether they want help. It's important for you to recognize the limits of what you can do to help, and it's important for them to take responsibility for their own life.

If It's an Emergency

If you think your friend's or roommate's problem has gone from a concern to an emergency, it can feel like a tremendous burden. You may not know what the right thing to do is, or how best to get help. In situations like this, you should not be the one deciding what to do. You should call health services, describe the problem, and ask them what they think should be done and what role you might play, if any. As always, offer to walk your friend or roommate to health services; if they say they don't need you to, you can say it would make you feel more comfortable if you did.

MOOD BOOSTERS

The big message of this chapter is this: if you think you might need help, go out and get it. In the meantime, and in addition, there are some things you can do on your own. They probably won't pull you out of a major—or even moderate—depression, but they can help boost your mood when you're down, help you manage everyday stress, and help keep your mind and body toned.

Before getting into what else helps, we should point out that in an important sense, this whole book is about mood boosters. Being aware of the Inside-Out Trap can help you to feel better about yourself. Avoiding irrationally negative thoughts about yourself and your future helps you to fight loneliness and to be less anxious. Understanding the J Curve makes getting things done less onerous and more appealing. Learning to deal more effectively with the tensions that arise with roommates, parents, friends, and social and academic life can make a huge difference in how you feel and how effectively you function.

Below are a few additional things that can make a big difference in your mood. They're no substitute for getting help when you need it, but they can help you stay healthy and balanced.

Exercise

Recent studies have found that regular cardiovascular exercise not only reduces stress, but can be as effective at boosting mood as Prozac. When you exercise, your brain releases happiness-producing endorphins to counterbalance the physical pain and exertion of exercise. Those happiness chemicals stick around even after you stop exercising.

Working out is itself an accomplishment you can feel good about no matter what else is going on in your life. A word to the wise, though: don't overdo it. Listen to your body. Especially if it's the first time you've gotten exercise in a while, begin slowly, keep at it, and work your way into shape over time. If you're having trouble getting started, remember the J Curve. The first couple of times might feel lousy, but within a few workouts, you'll start looking forward to it.

Sleep

We've said it before, but we'll say it again. Getting enough sleep really matters. Different people need different amounts, so make sure you're getting the amount you need (most people need around eight hours). Sleep deprivation can weaken your immune system and significantly impair your mental functioning. It can cause you to be less resilient in the face of stress and can cause depression. It's not a good cycle to get into.

If you find yourself unable to do everything you need to do during the course of an average day, your first inclination might be to skimp on sleep. But it's not an optional activity. You have to find something else to cut out of your schedule.

The guidelines for getting enough sleep can be tough to follow in a college environment, but still, they're useful to know. Go to bed at roughly the same time each night, and more important, wake up at the same time. Don't take long naps during the day. Don't exercise right before bed, don't drink alcohol (you might fall asleep for a while, but you're more likely to awaken during the night), and don't have caffeine after around 6:00 p.m., though different people react to caffeine differently. Remember, some soft drinks contain as much caffeine as about one-third of a cup of coffee. If you're feeling anxious about something and it's keeping you awake, get up and write it down. Once you know it's on paper, you're more likely to be able to let it go, at least long enough to fall asleep.

Being with People

According to one study, the best predictor of whether someone would become depressed after a bad event was whether they had at least one person in their lives they talked to almost every day. The people who had a close family member, friend, or significant other were much less likely to become depressed.

Having a busy social schedule is not a necessity, but having one or two good friends who you can really talk to is. You don't need to stay out all night partying, but time devoted to making friends and enhancing friendships is time well spent. So take some extra time at lunch to chat with friends, or take a break from work to visit a buddy upstairs, call your mom, or catch up with your best friend from home over IM.

Meditation

From: Rollo
To: Angel Applestein
Sent: Tuesday, November 9, 2:44 PM
Subject: oops

Dear Ms. Applestein:

I want to thank you for the excellent meditation class. As you could tell, I found it perhaps the most relaxing experience of my life. It was this extreme level of relaxation, rather than any intention to disturb, that caused my prolonged flatulence during the "Listen to the Quiet" exercise. Despite the temporary mayhem, I assure you that I heard the quiet, or at least some of it, and I would like you to reconsider your decision to ban me from future classes.

Mindfully yours,
Rollo

Rollo's experience notwithstanding, meditation has helped countless people lead more fulfilling lives. When researchers measured the brain activity of Tibetan monks while they were meditating, they found that the monks were the happiest people they had ever measured. Now, you might be thinking, "Well, yeah. I would be the happiest person ever if all I had to do was sit around all day." Fair enough. But similar studies have been done on students who had never tried meditation. The students found that their mood and sense of well-being improved, as did their physical health.

Meditating helps you discipline your mind in a way that allows you to gain some distance when frustrating and upsetting things happen. You can be aware of your reaction to the things around you without getting as tangled up in them. Over time, you may find that you are more relaxed in general and better able to cope with what life throws your way.

Learning to meditate is not hard, and it doesn't have to be practiced in connection with a particular set of religious beliefs or organizational affiliations. You can join a class or learn it from a friend or by reading a book; it can take as little as fifteen minutes a day.

Involvement in Something Bigger Than Yourself

Yes, your success and happiness in college come down to you—how much effort you put in; how you deal with change, setbacks, and uncertainty; how you treat the people around you; and how you manage your thoughts and feelings. But finding motivation, contentment, and especially meaning isn't just about you. It's about the world outside—outside yourself, and outside your campus.

That might mean getting involved in helping in the surrounding community—volunteering at a school, working at a homeless shelter, helping new immigrants gain access to local services. It might mean getting involved in a political cause that matters to you, or maintaining your connections to a religious community. It could mean joining a peer counseling group, starting a recycling and environmental awareness program on campus, or assisting a professor who works to resolve ethnic conflict around the world.

It's easy for your perspective to narrow, to become bogged down in the details and routines of college life. But when you pull yourself out of that orbit to discover the world around you and the positive impact you can have, you not only make your community or the world a better place, you'll feel more sane and grounded as you pursue what matters to you at college.

Epilogue

S ome of the ideas suggested in this book will be easy to implement. Calling your parents every few days isn't hard, nor is studying with a friend, talking with your roommate about the rules of the room, or going to a professor's office hours. Even though they're simple, each of these things can make a real difference in how you do and how you feel.

Other ideas will take more effort and patience, and maybe even a little courage. Talking to a professor if you feel overwhelmed by the workload can take courage, as can talking with your boyfriend or girlfriend about where you draw the line in your physical relationship, or talking with roommates about their eating issues or excessive drinking. Being honest with yourself about your sexuality can take courage, as can finding your niche after being cut from a team.

The setbacks and challenges will continue to come, but each one you take on makes the next one a little easier to handle. After all, the real secret to college—and to life—is not eliminating setbacks, but knowing you can handle them.

WHAT BECAME OF OUR STUDENTS after their freshman year?

Macani spent the summer working at the local ice cream shop and vowed never to eat ice cream again. She and Craig are still together but the divorce with ice cream persists.

PJ stayed on campus for the summer to coach a high school rowing camp. In the fall, she and Macani managed to get adjacent rooms in the sophomore dorms.

Sweeney was able to convince his father to let him lifeguard again for the summer, but spent a few evenings and weekends doing the filing at Uncle Frank's firm. Sweeney and Cube moved into the Sigma house in the fall.

Duncan spent the summer and subsequent fall semester in a work placement at an engineering firm. Sweeney sent him a steady supply of condolence pictures featuring the attractive women he met while lifeguarding.

Rollo got a summer job as an assistant meat inspector for the Food and Drug Administration. During his sophomore year, he rented an apartment with fellow members of the physics society. They proved to be in complete agreement on the poster front.

Appendix: Additional Resources

THE BEST RESOURCE: YOUR SCHOOL

The most important resources to tap into are those offered by *your* college. As soon as you arrive on campus, you should figure out what services are available to you and where they're located. Four key places to learn about are:

1. The office of the dean devoted to students (at your school, it might be called the Freshman Dean's Office, the Office of the Dean of Student Life, or some variation thereof)
2. The college health services office
3. The financial aid office
4. The registrar's office

Most of the programs and resources for students will originate in one of these four offices.

Many schools have other offices as well, devoted to things like studying, minority affairs, students with disabilities, women's issues, off-campus life, internships and jobs, and a host of other topics. Virtually every campus has affiliated religious resources, whether through an office of "united ministries" or through particular churches and temples.

Don't just read about these places; go visit them. Introduce yourself to the dean, and find out exactly where the health services are located in case of future emergency. Pick up brochures along the way, and ask lots of questions about what's available to you.

The Web is another great place to find resources. Most schools have their own site packed with information that ranges from campus maps and professors' e-mail addresses, to advice on a whole range of mental health concerns.

You should also get to know your residential advisor. That may be a dean or professor, or, more likely, a graduate student or upperclassman. Your advisor may be someone you feel comfortable turning to for important advice; and at the very least, advisors know lots of practical information and have had personal experiences that you can learn from.

LIST OF ADDITIONAL RESOURCES

Below, we offer a list of Web sites and books you may find helpful. The list is not intended to be comprehensive, but offers a good place to begin. All of the books mentioned can be obtained either at your school's library, in the campus bookstore, or through online stores like Amazon.com.

In General

The University of Buffalo has one of the most helpful Web sites we've found, at http://ub-counseling.buffalo.edu/vpc.html. It gathers online pamphlets from universities across North America on a whole range of campus topics, from studying to alcohol to contraception to mental health. If you have questions about a specific topic, this is a good place to start.

Another favorite general resource is *Feeling Good: The New Mood Therapy*, by David Burns (Avon, 1999). The field of cognitive therapy has heavily influenced the advice we give in this book. *Feeling Good* is the best general introduction to the field, and an outstanding advice book in its own right.

Making the Most of College: Students Speak Their Minds, by Richard Light (Harvard University Press, 2001), is one of the best books ever written about college life. It offers important findings from the author's research on academics, social life, advising, diversity, and other topics of interest to students, professors, and deans alike.

Doug's previous book, *Difficult Conversations: How to Discuss What Matters Most* (Penguin, 1999, with Bruce Patton and Sheila Heen), is another helpful resource. Geared toward a general audience, this book offers advice on how to raise and discuss tough issues, whether with a roommate, romantic partner, professor, parent, or friend.

Following are additional resources, listed by chapter.

CHAPTER 1: ROOMMATES

Getting to Yes: Negotiating Agreement Without Giving In, by Roger Fisher, William Ury, and Bruce Patton (Penguin, 1991).

http://www.residentassistant.com/advice/roommate1.htm
  This site offers specific questions to ask and discussions to
  have with your roommate.

CHAPTER 2: SOCIAL LIFE

*Painfully Shy: How to Overcome Social Anxiety and Reclaim
  Your Life,* by Barbara Markway and Gregory Markway
  (Pantheon Books, 1999).

Alcohol and Campus Culture

Substance Abuse Treatment Facility Locator:
  http://findtreatment.samhsa.gov/facilitylocatordoc.htm
  This site is set up by the Substance Abuse and Mental
  Health Services Administration, Department of Health and
  Human Services.

Harvard University Health Services—What to Do When a
  Friend Is Drunk:
  http://huhs.harvard.edu/HealthInformation/CWHC
  Wellness InformationAlcoholAndOtherDrugs.htm

Harvard School of Public Health, college alcohol study:
  http://www.hsph.harvard.edu/cas/About/index.html

National Institute on Alcohol Abuse and Alcoholism, fre-
  quently asked questions:
  http://www.niaaa.nih.gov/faq/faq.htm

National Institute on Alcohol Abuse and Alcoholism, statistics
  on college drinking:
  http://www.collegedrinkingprevention.gov/facts/snapshot.aspx

*Dying to Drink: Confronting Binge Drinking on College Cam-
  puses,* by Henry Wechsler and Bernice Wuethrich (Rodale
  Press, 2002).

CHAPTERS 3 AND 4:
ACADEMICS AND STUDYING

What Smart Students Know: Maximum Grades, Optimum Learning, Minimal Time, by Adam Robinson (Three Rivers Press, 1993).

Keys to College Studying: Becoming a Lifelong Learner, by Carol Carter, Joyce Bishop, and Sarah Lyman Kravits (Prentice Hall, 2002).

Emotional Intelligence: Why It Can Matter More Than IQ, by Daniel Goleman (Bantam, 1997).

Inside College: New Freedom, New Responsibility, by Henry Moses (College Board Publishing, 1991).

ADD and Learning Disabilities

Driven to Distraction: Recognizing and Coping with Attention Deficit Disorder from Childhood Through Adulthood, by Edward Hallowell and John Ratey (Touchstone Books, 1995).

College and Career Success for Students with Learning Disabilities, by Roslyn Dolber (McGraw-Hill, 1996).

Learning Outside the Lines: Two Ivy League Students with Learning Disabilities and ADHD Give You the Tools for Academic Success and Educational Revolution, by Jonathan Mooney and David Cole (Fireside, 2000).

CHAPTER 5: IDENTITY
Race and Ethnicity

An extraordinary number of good books are available on race, ethnicity, immigration, religion, and minority experiences in

America, ranging from novels and autobiographical stories to sociological and economic studies. This list is just a tiny sampling and doesn't begin to exhaust the range of topics and experiences:

A *Testament of Hope: The Essential Writings and Speeches of Martin Luther King, Jr.,* by Martin Luther King, Jr. James M. Washington, editor (Harper San Francisco, 1990).

Hunger of Memory: The Education of Richard Rodriguez, by Richard Rodriguez (Bantam, 1983).

Asian American Dreams: The Emergence of an American People, by Helen Zia (Farrar, Straus & Giroux, 2001).

Why Are All the Black Kids Sitting Together in the Cafeteria? And Other Conversations About Race, by Beverly Daniel Tatum (Basic Books, 1999).

Half and Half: Writers on Growing Up Biracial and Bicultural, Claudine O'Hearn, editor (Pantheon Books, 1998).

Crossing Customs: International Students Write on U.S. College Life and Culture, Andrew Garrod and Jay Davis, editors (Garland Publishing, 1999).

In the Name of Identity: Violence and the Need to Belong, by Amin Maalouf (Penguin, 2003).

Illiberal Education: The Politics of Race and Sex on Campus, by Dinesh D'Souza (Free Press, 1998).

Sister Outsider: Essays and Speeches, by Audre Lorde (The Crossing Press, 1984).

Sexual Orientation

College and University Campus GBLT Organizations, list of campus organizations:

http://www.dv-8.com/resources/us/local/campus.html

Gay Student Center, Web community and resources:
http://gaystudentcenter.studentcenter.org

Out on Fraternity Row: Personal Accounts of Being Gay in a College Fraternity, Shane Windmeyer and Pamela Freeman, editors (Alyson, 1998).

Secret Sisters: Stories of Being Lesbian and Bisexual in a College Sorority, by Shane Windmeyer and Pamela Freeman (Alyson, 2001).

Out and About Campus: Personal Accounts by Lesbian, Gay, Bisexual, and Transgendered College Students, Kim Howard and Annie Stevens, editors (Alyson, 2000).

Disabilities

The Disability Studies Reader, by Lennard J. Davis (Routledge, 1997).

Transition to Postsecondary Education: Strategies for Students with Disabilities, by Kristine Wiest Webb (Pro Ed, 2000).

Gender

In a Different Voice: Psychological Theory and Women's Development, by Carol Gilligan (Harvard University Press, 1993).

Making Connections: The Relational Worlds of Adolescent Girls at Emma Willard School, Carol Gilligan, Nona Lyons, and Trudy Hanmer, editors (Harvard University Press, 1990).

Real Boys: Rescuing Our Sons from the Myths of Boyhood, by William Pollack (Owl Books, 1999).

Gender on Campus: Issues for College Women, by Sharon Gmelch and Marcie Heffernan Stoffer (Rutgers University Press, 1998).

CHAPTER 6: RELATIONSHIPS

University of Texas at Austin—Romantic Relationships in College:
http://www.utexas.edu/student/cmhc/booklets/romrelations/romrelations.html

The Worst-Case Scenario Survival Handbook: Dating and Sex, by Joshua Piven, David Borgenicht, and Jennifer Worick (Chronicle Books, 2001).

Dating 101: The Instant Cure for Romance Blues, by Melissa Darnay and Zella Case (Splash of Ink, 2002).

How to Break Your Addiction to a Person, by Howard Halpern (Bantam, 2003).

Dating for Dummies, by Joy Browne (For Dummies, 1997).

CHAPTER 7: SEX
STDs

Centers for Disease Control, fact sheet on sexually transmitted diseases:
http://www.cdc.gov/nchstp/dstd/disease_info.htm

Contraception and Pregnancy

Planned Parenthood, contraception, pregnancy, abortion, women's health:
http://www.plannedparenthood.org/health

Emergency Contraception:
http://ec.princeton.edu

National Women's Health Information Center:
http://www.4woman.gov

Pregnancy Center (1-800-395-HELP), provides support and offers information:

http://www.pregnancycenters.org

Rape and Sexual Abuse

SurviveRape.org helps survivors and those supporting survivors after an assault:

http://www.SurviveRape.org

Rape, Abuse, and Incest National Network:

http://www.rainn.org

National Library of Medicine, information on rape and coping:

http://www.nlm.nih.gov/medlineplus/rape.html

Male Survivor, information for male survivors of sexual abuse:

http://www.malesurvivor.org

I Never Called It Rape: The Ms. Report on Recognizing, Fighting, and Surviving Date and Acquaintance Rape, by Robin Warshaw (Perennial, 1994).

CHAPTER 8: PARENTS

Letting Go: A Parent's Guide to Understanding the College Years, by Karen Levin Coburn and Madge Lawrence Treeger (Perennial, 1997).

Don't Tell Me What to Do, Just Send Money: The Essential Parenting Guide to the College Years, by Helen Johnson and Christine Schelhas-Miller (Griffin Trade Paperback, 2000).

CHAPTER 9: MENTAL HEALTH

Suicide Hotlines

Suicide Hotlines lists national and local suicide hotline numbers:
http://suicidehotlines.com

The Aware Foundation, suicide, depression, and mental health hotlines:
http://www.awarefoundation.org/aware/resources/suicide_hotlines.asp

Center for Suicide Prevention, information if someone you know is suicidal:
http://www.suicideinfo.ca/csp/go.aspx?tabid=75

Depression and Anxiety

Feeling Good: The New Mood Therapy, by David Burns (Avon, 1999).

Beating the College Blues, by Paul Grayson and Philip Meilman (Checkmark Books, 1999).

The Noonday Demon: An Atlas of Depression, by Andrew Solomon (Scribner, 2002).

The Anxiety and Phobia Workbook, by Edmund J. Bourne (New Harbinger, 2000).

Authentic Happiness: Using the New Positive Psychology to Realize Your Potential for Lasting Fulfillment, by Martin Seligman (Free Press, 2004).

College of the Overwhelmed: The Campus Mental Health Crisis and What to Do About It, by Richard D. Kadison (Jossey-Bass, 2004).

The 100 Simple Secrets of Happy People, by David Niven (Harper, 2000).

Eating Concerns

Surviving an Eating Disorder: Strategies for Family and Friends, by Michelle Siegel (Perennial, 1997).

Sensing the Self: Women's Recovery from Bulimia, by Sheila Reindl (Harvard University Press, 2002).

The Body Image Workbook: An 8-Step Program for Learning to Like Your Looks, by Thomas Cash (New Harbinger, 1997).

Anatomy of a Food Addiction: The Brain Chemistry of Overeating: An Effective Program to Overcome Compulsive Eating, by Anne Katherine (Gurze Books, 1997).

The Ultimate Weight Solution: The 7 Keys to Weight Loss Freedom, by Phil McGraw (Free Press, 2003).

Addiction

See also listings under Chapter 2: Social Life.

Centers for Disease Control—Guide to Quitting Smoking:
http://www.cdc.gov/tobacco/how2quit.htm

Alcoholics Anonymous:
http://www.alcoholics-anonymous.org

Sober for Good: New Solutions for Drinking Problems— Advice from Those Who Have Succeeded, by Anne M. Fletcher (Houghton Mifflin, 2002).

Willpower's Not Enough: Recovering from Addictions of Every Kind, by Arnold M. Washton (Perennial, 1990).

Trauma

Trauma and Recovery, by Judith Herman (Basic Books, 1992).

When Bad Things Happen to Good People, by Harold S. Kushner (Avon, 1983).

Meditation

The Relaxation Response, by Herbert Benson and Miriam Klipper (HarperTorch, 1976).

The Miracle of Mindfulness, by Thich Nhat Hanh (Beacon, 1999).

OTHER PRACTICAL TIPS

The College Board—Packing List:
http://www.collegeboard.com/article/0,3868,2-10-0-9763,00.html

Askmen.com—How to Do Laundry:
http://www.askmen.com/fashion/how_to/9_how_to.html

How to Clean a Bathroom:
http://msms.essortment.com/cleanthebathro_reie.htm

For tips on how to get involved with campus recycling and related activities, check out:
http://ulsf.org/cgi-bin/searchresults.cfm?catlD=11&subcatlD=38

Paying for College Without Going Broke, The Princeton Review (Princeton Review, 2003).

The Healthy College Cookbook, by Alexandra Nimetz, Jason Stanley, and Emeline Starr (Storey, 1999).

The Better Homes and Gardens New Cookbook, BH&G Editors (Meredith Books, 2002).

Index

Future
  fearing catastrophic, 59–61
  grades and, 53, 56–57

G

Gays. *See* Sexual orientation
Gender, 229
  communication about sex and,
    149–52
Grades, 52–53
  extracurricular activities and, 38
  first semester, 73
  future and, 56–57
  parental control and, 183–85
  poor
    blaming others for, 61–62
    coping with, 58–59
    keeping in perspective, 59–61
  self-image and, 53–56

H

Herpes, 157
HIV/AIDS, 157–58
Homosexuality. *See* Sexual orienta-
  tion
"Hooking up," 153
Human papillomavirus (HPV),
  156

I

Idealization, 119–21
Identity
  challenge of, 98–99
  parental relationship and, 186–87
  race and ethnicity and, 99, 227–29
    accepting complexity, 100–101
    internal *versus* external expecta-
      tions, 101–2
    personal experiences and, 102–5
  sexual orientation, 105
    coming out, 108–10

  coming out *versus* staying in,
    107–8
  self-discovery, 106
  thought, *versus* action, 115
  understanding, 97–98
Infatuation, 119–23
  flirting online and, 127–28
Insecurities
  comparing self to others and, 23–27
  first impressions and, 3
  roommate pairings and, 4–5
Inside-Out Trap, 23–27
  talking about sexual experiences
    and, 142–45
Inspiration, studying and, 79
Instant messaging, flirting with,
  124–28
Intelligence, grades and, 54–56
Internal lives, social anxiety and,
  23–27
Involvement, in outside world,
  218–19

J

J curve, 77–79, 82

L

Law, drugs and drinking and, 44–45
Learning disabilities, 227
Life success, grades and, 56–57
Light, Richard, 38
Loneliness, coping with, 31–34
Loss, coping with, 204–5

M

Majors, 70–73
*Making the Most of College: Stu-
  dents Speak Their Minds,* 225
Masturbation, 155–56
Medication. *See also* Contraceptives
  mental health treatment, 210